How to Cook Everything™

Quick Cooking

Other Books by Mark Bittman:

How to Cook Everything™

How to Cook Everything™: Vegetarian Cooking

How to Cook Everything™: Holiday Cooking

How to Cook Everything™: Easy Weekend Cooking

How to Cook Everything™: The Basics

The Minimalist Cooks at Home

The Minimalist Cooks Dinner

The Minimalist Entertains

Fish: The Complete Guide to Buying and Cooking

Leafy Greens

With Jean-Georges Vongerichten:

Simple to Spectacular

Jean-Georges: Cooking at Home with a Four-Star Chef

How to Cook *Everything*™

Quick Cooking

Mark Bittman

Illustrations by Alan Witschonke

WILEY

Wiley Publishing, Inc.

Published by Wiley Publishing, Inc., Hoboken, NJ

For general information on our other products and services or to obtain technical support please contact our Customer Care Department within the U.S. at 800-762-2974, outside the U.S. at 317-572-3993 or fax 317-572-4002.

Wiley also publishes its books in a variety of electronic formats. Some content that appears in print may not be available in electronic books.

Library of Congress Cataloging-in-Publication Data:

Bittman, Mark.
How to cook everything. Quick cooking / Mark Bittman ; illustrations
by Alan Witschonke.— 1st ed.
    p. cm.
ISBN 0-7645-2511-5 (Paperback : alk. paper)
1. Quick and easy cookery. I. Title: Quick cooking. II. Title.
TX833.5.B55 2003
641.5'55—dc21
                       2003008737

Manufactured in the United States of America

10 9 8 7 6 5 4 3 2 1

For my parents and my kids

WILEY PUBLISHING, INC.

Publisher: Natalie Chapman

Executive Editor: Anne Ficklen

Senior Editor: Linda Ingroia

Production Editor: M. Faunette Johnston

Cover Design: Cecelia Diskin

Book Design: Edwin Kuo and Anthony Bagliani, Solid Design

Interior Layout: Nick Anderson

Manufacturing Buyer: Kevin Watt

Contents

Acknowledgments   vi

About This Book   vii

What to Know About Quick Cooking   viii

1   *Starters*   1

2   *Pasta*   17

3   *Fish*   33

4   *Poultry*   49

5   *Meat*   63

6   *Rice and Beans*   83

7   *Vegetables*   93

8   *Desserts*   105

Quick Menus   112

Recipes That Take 20 Minutes or Less   114

Tips Reference   116

Index   123

Conversions, Substitutions, and Helpful Hints   131

Acknowledgments

I have been writing about food for nearly 25 years, and it's impossible to thank all the people who have helped me make a go of it during that time. Most of them know who they are—we have shared cooking, eating, and talking, much of what constitutes my life—and together I do owe them a broad "thanks."

However, some special friends and colleagues have been there for me and helped me out in recent years, and I want to thank them especially: Mitchell Orfuss, Naomi Glauberman, John Bancroft, Madeline Meacham, David Paskin, Pamela Hort, Jack Hitt, Semeon Tsalbins, Susan Moldow, Bill Shinker, Jim Nelson, Fred Zolna, Sherry Slade, Lisa Sanders, Genevieve Ko, Charlie Pinsky, Geof Drummond, Sam Sifton, Nancy Cobb, and Steve Rubin.

I have been blessed, too, with great colleagues at Wiley: Linda Ingroia, who has worked tirelessly on the new *How to Cook Everything*™ series; Edwin Kuo, Jeffrey Faust, Cecelia Diskin, and Holly Wittenberg for great covers and interiors; Faunette Johnston, the production editor, and Christina Van Camp for keeping keen eyes on clarity and consistency; and Kate Fischer and Michele Sewell for managing *How to Cook Everything* publicity opportunities. Jennifer Feldman got the *How to Cook Everything* series up and running and Natalie Chapman and Robert Garber have given it tremendous support. My agent, Angela Miller, is simply the best, and has been a terrific influence in my life for over a decade; huge thanks to her, as always.

Few of my cookbooks would have been written without the help and inspiration of Karen Baar, to whom I remain grateful. And, as always, special thanks to my fabulous children, Kate and Emma, and my most frequent companions, John H. Willoughby, John Ringwald, and Alisa X. Smith, all of whom give me invaluable love and perspective on a daily basis, and newfound confidence in the world of cooking.

How to Cook Everything™: Quick Cooking is intended to be a useful collection of my favorite quick recipes—those that take 30 minutes or less to prepare. There was a time when "quick" cooking meant an hour or less—Pierre Franey's *New York Times* column "The 60-Minute Gourmet" was an integral part of America's culinary coming of age—but standards have changed. Like almost everything else in life, cooking must be faster and more efficient than ever before.

Thirty-minute dishes allow you to enjoy simple and doable dinners, lunches, brunches, and snacks when you don't have much time to spend in the kitchen, and they keep you from relying too heavily on fast food, take-out, and prepared supermarket meals— none of which are reliably good, and all of which are questionable nutritionally.

Like almost all the recipes I make, those here usually can be varied to your taste, diet, or pantry—what's available to cook is often more of a determining factor than what you want to eat—so consider this book a guide for specific meals but, more importantly, a springboard for your own creativity. In addition to more than 90 basic recipes, there are dozens of variations, as well as shopping, preparation, and cooking tips. There are also lists of quick ideas, and illustrations for the most useful or trickiest techniques. The fastest recipes—those that take only 20 minutes or less to cook—are labeled with an 🕐 icon.

If you're looking for ideas for complete meals, see pages 112 to 113, where there are 18 weeknight, seasonal, special occasion, and healthful menus. (The menus are simply food pairings of recipes in this book; they are not guaranteed to be made within 30 minutes although they are fast meals.)

When it comes to quick cooking, I imagine your goals and mine are the same—to make good food without dedicating a lot of time and effort to it. This book can help you do that.

What to Know About Quick Cooking

The goal for many cooks these days is to put something together as quickly as possible—even in 10 or 20 minutes. Although many dishes here meet that goal, the scope for this book is 30 minutes, to allow you to prepare meals with a balance of cooking styles and a variety of flavors, so you don't get bored, give up trying to make real meals, and order out. There are not, after all, a great deal of 10- or 15-minute recipes.

With this collection, I have made some judgment calls and some assumptions. When a preparation time is given as "30 minutes," it always means roughly 30 minutes— your skills, kitchen setup, and ingredients will all affect timing. I include grilled foods here, for example, even though starting a charcoal fire takes about a half hour; you can always plan a little ahead, use a gas grill, stovetop grill pan, or the broiler. I make some other assumptions, too: bean dishes, for example, are quick to prepare as long as you have cooked (or canned) beans, so I've included them although, obviously, if you have to cook beans from scratch they don't fit in the time parameter.

Nor should you expect to cook too many complete meals using two or three recipes from this book; start with one recipe, and augment it with simple salads or store-bought items, like bread or dessert.

Cooking Basics

Here are some thoughts and guidelines on efficient, safe, and smart cooking in general and on quick cooking in particular.

Time

Quick cooking is basic, simple cooking. It takes no more time to cook many meals than it does to call for a pizza and pick it up, or even wait for it to be delivered. Grilling a piece of meat or fish and steaming a vegetable or preparing a salad is a 20-minute operation; so is making a simple pasta dish.

It's easy to have the makings of a quick meal on hand just by maintaining the right mix of staples. Certain foods belong in every kitchen all the time, and keep nearly indefinitely.

To stock your pantry and refrigerator, make sure you have on hand:

- pasta and other grains, especially rice
- canned beans and other vegetables, especially tomatoes
- spices, and dried herbs when fresh are unavailable
- liquid seasonings such as olive oil, vinegar, and soy sauce
- eggs and butter
- flour, cornmeal, and the like
- nuts and dried fruits
- onions, potatoes, garlic, and other long-keeping vegetables
- non-fat dried milk (usually for emergencies)
- canned or boxed broth

With this list alone you will be equipped to make literally dozens of different meals, from pancakes to pasta. When you throw in the fresh ingredients that you're likely to have in the refrigerator as a result of weekly shopping jaunts—vegetables, herbs, fruit, meat, fish, milk, cheese, and other perishables—the result is that you'll be able to prepare most of the 90+ recipes in this book without going out to search for special ingredients.

In general, I consider whole, fresh ingredients a priority. Of course, when time is an issue, I am not against the use of store-bought broth, or frozen spinach, as part of a recipe, especially where the ordinary-at-best nature of such products is disguised by the other ingredients in the recipe. But I do not believe in "miracle" recipes based on canned or dried soups, artificial mayonnaise, or powdered desserts. This is a cookbook, not a chemistry class; to cook good dishes you must start with real food. In general, the better the ingredients you have the simpler your cooking can be.

A word about recipe timing. The timing for every recipe is always approximate. The rate at which food cooks is dependent on the moisture content and temperature of the food itself; measurements (which are rarely perfectly accurate); heat level (everyone's "medium-high" heat is not the same, and most ovens are off by at least 25°F in one direction or another); the kind of equipment (some pans conduct heat better than others); even the air temperature. So be sure to use time as a rough guideline, and judge doneness by touch, sight, and taste.

Food Safety

Even if you're short on time, you shouldn't cut corners with food safety. Begin by keeping your hands and all food preparation surfaces and utensils perfectly clean; soap and hot water are good enough, although the new antibacterial kitchen soaps are probably even better. Wash cutting boards after using, and don't prepare food directly on your counters unless you wash them as well. Change sponges frequently, too, and throw your sponges in the washing machine whenever you wash clothes in hot water.

Change your kitchen towel frequently also—at least once a day. Cook food to the proper degree of doneness. (Sometimes, there's a conflict between "proper degree of doneness" and the best-tasting results, and in those instances it's a judgment call, which must be made by you.)

Techniques

The quickest food is raw, but it's usually not the best tasting, and some people aren't comfortable eating raw foods. By combining ingredients using the same technique—grilling meat and vegetables at the same time, for example, or making a quick stew—you can get a whole meal on the table quickly. But generally speaking, the quickest techniques are broiling and sautéing pan-cooking where there is no oven preheat time, no grill start up, no boiling of water—you just start cooking.

The challenges of broiling and sautéing are that they require using cuts of meat or fish that become (or remain) tender without the long, slow cooking that softens tougher cuts. My recipes specify which cuts to use for best results, and I recommend you stick with them.

A once-famous French chef named Edouard de Pomiane, wrote a book called *French Cooking in Ten Minutes*. Most of the recipes took far longer than that—or required that you had things on hand such as fresh tomato sauce—but he did have some great advice, a piece of which I'll paraphrase: As soon as you enter the kitchen, start a pot of water to boil. I don't know what you'll use it for, but you'll use it.

You may know you don't need the water, in which case by all means don't start it. But the point is this: Take care of the little, simple things in the kitchen—think ahead—and the big things will become easier.

Equipment

Equipment for quick cooking and normal cooking are about the same, with a couple of exceptions. There are two or three gadgets that make quick cooking quicker: One is a mandoline, a simple slicing device that allows you to make quick work of vegetables; even if your knife skills are good, a mandoline is nice to have, and an inexpensive one costs less than $30. The other is a food processor, a marvel of efficiency.

And although I prefer charcoal grills to gas grills—there is nothing like cooking over real charcoal—the fact that gas grills can be preheated, with no effort, in just a few minutes, is a major contribution to fast outdoor cooking. Indoor electric grills are another good, fast option.

The Last Word

People become obsessed with food and cooking; I have been obsessed with it for all of my adult life. But as time goes on I realize that—as one of my older daughter's bedtime books was titled—*Simple Things Are Best*.

It's true. Each year, I experiment less and less with complex dishes, and try to master the simple staples both of our widely divergent culture, and of other cultures from around the world. I look for good ingredients, and handle them minimally. I am usually satisfied with the food I prepare, but I am the first to admit that it is very rarely on the same level as that served in the world's best restaurants. (It's better, however, than that served in the vast majority of restaurants.)

Striving for brilliance in everyday cooking is a recipe for frustration, but achieving good, simple meals quickly is something anyone can do. This book will put you on your way.

1 | Starters

Great Green Salad   2

   Vinaigrette   3

   Quick Blue Cheese Dressing   3

Cabbage and Carrot Salad with Soy-Lime Dressing   4

Greens with Bacon   5

Omelet   6

Frittata   8

Cheese Quesadillas   9

Mushroom Soup   10

Kale and Potato Soup   11

Corn, Tomato, and Zucchini Soup with Basil   12

Black Bean Soup   13

Quick Chicken Soup with Rice or Noodles   14

Lightning-Quick Fish Soup   15

20 minutes or less

Great Green Salad

When you are in a hurry, a salad can be as simple or complex as you have time to make it. Almost any combination of greens can be used, and your dressing can be freshly squeezed lemon juice or vinegar, olive oil, and salt and fresh pepper, all to taste; a more flavorful vinaigrette; or something richer and more satisfying like Quick Blue Cheese Dressing (at right).

Makes 4 servings

Time: 10 minutes

4 to 6 cups torn assorted greens (trimmed, washed, and dried)

1/4 to 1/3 cup extra-virgin olive oil or walnut oil

1 or 2 tablespoons balsamic vinegar or sherry vinegar

Pinch salt, plus more to taste

Freshly ground black pepper to taste (optional)

Place the greens in a bowl and drizzle them with oil, vinegar, and a pinch of salt. Toss and taste. Correct seasoning, add pepper if desired, and serve immediately.

Shopping Tip: Any greens, as long as they're tender enough, can be used in salads. If you were to pick only one, romaine makes the most sense: It's got both tender and crunchy parts, and it is slightly but not too bitter. These days, you can buy "mesclun" assortments either in bulk or in packages, in almost every super-market. They're colorful, flavorful, often organic, and usually quite fresh; the only downside is that they tend to be expensive.

5 Quick Additions to Salads

1 Any nuts or seeds, crumbled or chopped if necessary

2 The leaves of fresh herbs, torn into pieces

3 Sliced pears, apples, or other fruit

4 Very thinly sliced Parmesan (use a vegetable peeler to produce thin curls) or other hard cheese

5 Diced roasted red or yellow peppers (or canned pimentos), olives, capers, or anchovies

Simple Greek Salad A bright-tasting salad. Toss together 4 to 6 cups torn mixed greens (at least some should be strong-tasting) with 1/4 cup cleaned and chopped radish; 1/4 cup minced fresh mint leaves or mint mixed with parsley; 1/4 cup chopped feta cheese, or more to taste; and 1/4 cup pitted and chopped black olives. Drizzle with olive oil and freshly squeezed lemon juice to taste.

Arugula and Blue Cheese Salad Top 4 to 6 cups torn arugula with a crumbling of blue cheese, preferably Roquefort, Gorgonzola, or Stilton. Add 1/2 cup pitted and roughly chopped black olives. Use olive oil and freshly squeezed lemon juice for dressing.

Vinaigrette

Makes 1 cup • Time: 5 minutes

Emulsified vinaigrettes are only important if you care. Sometimes that extra creaminess is nice (and an immersion blender works brilliantly). But usually it doesn't matter much; I just toss everything in a bowl and whisk it for 30 seconds or so.

1/4 cup good vinegar, such as sherry, balsamic, or high-quality red or white wine, plus more to taste

1/2 teaspoon salt, plus more if needed

1/2 teaspoon Dijon mustard (optional)

3/4 cup extra-virgin olive oil, plus more if needed

2 teaspoons minced shallots (optional)

Freshly ground black pepper to taste

1 Briefly mix the vinegar, salt, and optional mustard with an immersion blender, food processor or blender, or with a fork or wire whisk.

2 Slowly add the oil in a stream (drop by drop if whisking) until an emulsion forms; or just whisk everything together briefly. Add the remaining oil faster, but still in a stream.

3 Taste to adjust salt and add more oil or vinegar if needed. Add the shallots and pepper. This is best made fresh but will keep, refrigerated, for a few days; bring back to room temperature before using.

Quick Blue Cheese Dressing

Makes about 1 cup • Time: 5 minutes

This is a sharp, creamy, and rich salad dressing, a real classic. Add 1/4 teaspoon or so of minced garlic if you want to make it even more pungent. Great as a dip for vegetables, too.

1/2 cup crumbled Roquefort or other blue cheese, such as Stilton, Maytag blue, or Gorgonzola

1/2 cup sour cream or plain yogurt

Freshly squeezed lemon juice as needed

Salt and freshly ground black pepper to taste

1 Combine the cheese and sour cream or yogurt in a small bowl, mashing with a fork; the mixture should remain somewhat lumpy.

2 Add enough lemon juice to give a creamy consistency. Add salt if necessary and a bit of pepper. This dressing keeps fairly well, refrigerated, for a few days.

5 Quick Additions to Vinaigrette

1 Any fresh or dried herb, in small proportions, usually less than 1 teaspoon (fresh), or just a pinch of dried per cup

2 Soy sauce, Worcestershire sauce, or other liquid seasonings, as much as 1 tablespoon per cup

3 Honey or other sweeteners, from 1 teaspoon to 1 tablespoon per cup

4 Whole grain mustards, 1 teaspoon to 1 tablespoon per cup. Or dry mustard, about 1/2 teaspoon per cup

5 Cayenne, crushed red pepper flakes, or minced fresh chiles, from a pinch to 1/2 teaspoon per cup

Cabbage and Carrot Salad with Soy-Lime Dressing

A nice, Asian-style variation on the simple green salad, highlighted by the wonderful lime-and-soy based vinaigrette, which is likely to become a part of your standard repertoire.

Makes 4 servings

Time: 15 minutes

---

1 pound napa or savoy cabbage, cored and shredded (below)

2 carrots, peeled and grated

2 or 3 scallions, minced

¼ to ⅓ cup peanut (preferred) or canola oil

2 tablespoons freshly squeezed lime juice

1 teaspoon soy sauce

Salt and freshly ground black pepper to taste

Combine the vegetables. Whisk together the oil, lime juice, and soy; taste and add salt and pepper if necessary. Toss the dressing with the vegetables and serve.

Shopping Tips: Peanut oil is not an all-purpose oil, but it's great for frying, and it's also wonderful when you want to give a distinctively Asian twist to almost anything.

When shopping for soy sauce, look for ingredients in this order: soy, wheat (wheat followed by soy is also acceptable), and salt. If the first ingredient is salt, and a chemical is listed in the ingredient list, it isn't real soy sauce.

Coring and Shredding Cabbage

1  2 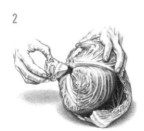 3  4

(Steps 1–2) The easiest way to core a head cabbage is to cut a small cone-shaped section from the bottom, then remove it. **(Step 3)** To shred head cabbage, first cut it into manageable pieces. **(Step 4)** Cut thin sections across the head; they'll naturally fall into shreds. If the shreds are too long, just cut across them.

Greens with Bacon

This is an unusual take on salads, but greens with good bacon is one of the great food combinations ever. Best served warm—no one wants cold bacon, but furthermore, the warm bacon will wilt and tenderize the greens slightly, a nice touch.

Makes 4 servings

Time: About 30 minutes

2 tablespoons olive oil

About ½ pound best slab bacon you can find, cut into ½-inch cubes

1 tablespoon chopped shallot

4 cups torn dandelion or other bitter greens, such as arugula, watercress, or frisée, or a combination of any salad greens (trimmed, washed, and dried)

About ¼ cup top-quality red wine vinegar

1 teaspoon Dijon mustard

Salt and freshly ground black pepper to taste

1 Place the olive oil in a skillet and turn the heat to medium. Add the bacon and cook slowly until it is crisp all over, 10 minutes or more. Add the shallot and cook a minute or two longer, until the shallot softens. Keep the bacon warm in the skillet.

2 Heat a salad bowl by filling it with hot water and letting it sit for a minute. Dry it and toss in the greens. Add the vinegar and mustard to the skillet, and bring just to a boil, stirring. Pour the liquid and the bacon over the greens, season to taste (it shouldn't need much salt), and serve immediately.

Shopping Tip: Slab bacon is not only usually of higher quality than presliced bacon, it keeps longer, and it can be cut into chunks, a desirable option for flavor and texture in some dishes.

Master this technique and you'll never be without a quick lunch or supper again. The butter (or oil, if you prefer) is an integral part of the flavor of this creation; don't skimp unless you must.

Makes 2 servings

Time: 10 minutes

2 tablespoons plus 1 teaspoon butter (you can use less with a non-stick pan, or substitute extra-virgin olive oil)

4 or 5 eggs

2 tablespoons milk or cream

Salt and freshly ground black pepper to taste

1 Place the 2 tablespoons butter in a medium-to-large skillet, preferably non-stick, and turn the heat to medium-high. Beat together the eggs and milk or cream, just until blended; add salt and pepper to taste.

2 When the butter melts, swirl it around the pan until its foam subsides, then pour in the egg mixture. Cook undisturbed for about 30 seconds, then use a fork or thin-bladed spatula to push the edges of the eggs toward the center. As you do this, tip the pan to allow the uncooked eggs in the center to reach the perimeter.

3 Repeat until the omelet is still moist but no longer runny, a total of about 3 minutes. If you prefer, you can even stop cooking a little sooner, when there are still some runny eggs in the center; most of this will cook from the heat retained by the eggs, and you'll have a moister omelet.

4 Use a large spatula to fold the omelet in half or in thirds and place it on a plate. Rub the top of the omelet with the remaining teaspoon of butter and serve.

Cooking Tip: Once, omelets were difficult to make, and required a lot of fat to keep from sticking. The non-stick pan changed that. With it, you can make an omelet successfully, on the first try, with a minimum of fat. If you want to make omelets for one, get a 6- or 8-inch skillet; for larger omelets, use a 10- or 12-inch skillet.

Mushroom Omelet Before cooking the omelet, sauté 1 cup minced mushrooms in 2 tablespoons butter or oil in a small skillet over medium-high heat until softened, about 10 minutes. Sprinkle with salt and pepper and finish with 1 tablespoon of cream (optional). Make the omelet, keeping the mushrooms warm. Place the mushrooms across one side of the egg mixture just before it is completely set. Fold the other side over and finish as above.

Spanish Omelet Before cooking the omelet, melt 1 tablespoon butter in a small saucepan over medium heat. Add 2 tablespoons minced scallion or onion and cook for 30 seconds. Stir in 1 cup chopped tomatoes and cook for about 2 minutes. Season with salt and pepper and keep warm. Make the omelet, placing the filling across one side of the egg mixture just before it is completely set. Fold the other side over and finish as above.

Western Omelet More like a frittata (page 8), but nevertheless an American tradition. In Step 2, when the butter melts, add to it 2 tablespoons each minced bell pepper (preferably red), onion, and ham. Cook for 2 minutes, stirring, before adding the eggs and proceeding as above.

5 Quick Fillings for Omelets

Use these fillings alone or in combination, but don't exceed about 1 cup of filling for an omelet this size.

1 Grated cheese

2 Any cooked and diced vegetable (leftovers are fine, whether steamed, boiled, or sautéed; rinse with boiling water before using if necessary to remove unwanted flavors)

3 Minced ham, crisp-cooked bacon, sausage meat, or other chopped meat

4 Minced fresh herbs, preferably a combination of 2 tablespoons parsley, 1 tablespoon each chervil and chives, and $1/2$ teaspoon tarragon (all chopped), but you can adjust this according to taste

5 Cooked seafood, such as shrimp, scallops, or crabmeat, shredded or minced

Frittata

The basic frittata—or egg pie—is very much like the basic omelet, but even easier to master, although it does take longer to make. The variations may be used singly or in combination, but they spring from this basic recipe.

Makes 4 servings

Time: About 30 minutes

2 tablespoons butter or olive oil

5 or 6 eggs

1/2 cup freshly grated Parmesan or other cheese

Salt and freshly ground black pepper to taste

Minced fresh parsley leaves for garnish

1 Preheat the oven to 350°F.

2 Place the butter or oil in a medium-to-large ovenproof skillet, preferably non-stick, and turn the heat to medium. While it's heating, beat together the eggs, cheese, salt, and pepper. When the butter melts or the oil is hot, pour the eggs into the skillet and turn the heat to medium-low. Cook, undisturbed, for about 10 minutes, or until the bottom of the frittata is firm.

3 Transfer the skillet to the oven. Bake, checking every 5 minutes or so, just until the top of the frittata is no longer runny, 10 to 20 minutes more. (To speed things up, turn on the broiler, but be very careful not to overcook.) Garnish and serve hot or at room temperature.

Vegetable Frittata Stir about 1 cup cooked and roughly chopped broccoli, asparagus, spinach, chard, or kale into the egg mixture just before turning it into the skillet. Proceed as above.

Herb Frittata Mince about 1 cup of fresh herbs—chervil, parsley, dill, or basil should make up the bulk of them, but others such as tarragon, oregano, marjoram, or chives may be added in smaller quantities—and stir them into the egg mixture just before turning it into the skillet. Proceed as above, garnishing with whatever fresh herb you like.

Cheese Quesadillas

You can assemble all four quesadillas at once, then wrap and refrigerate them until you're ready to cook. (The cooking takes almost no time.) If you prefer, dry-sauté these with no oil at all, in a non-stick or well-seasoned cast-iron skillet.

Makes 8 to 16 servings

Time: 15 minutes

4 tablespoons vegetable oil (optional)

8 (8-inch) flour tortillas

1½ cups grated Cheddar, Jack, or other cheese, or a combination

½ cup minced scallion

½ cup minced canned (not too hot) green chiles

¼ cup Tomato-Onion Salsa (page 81) or any salsa (optional)

1 The easiest way to make these is to build them in the skillet. So: Place 1 tablespoon of oil, if you're using it, in a medium skillet and turn the heat to medium. A minute later, place a tortilla in the skillet. Top with a quarter of the cheese, scallion, chiles, and salsa (if you are using it), then with another tortilla.

2 Cook about 2 minutes, or until the cheese begins to melt. Turn and cook another 2 to 3 minutes, until the cheese is melted and both sides are toasted. Drain if necessary, then cut into wedges and serve, or keep warm until the remaining quesadillas are done.

3 Additions to Quesadillas

1 Grilled chicken
2 Cooked beans or mushrooms
3 Mashed ripe avocado

Mushroom Soup

Make this with plain button mushrooms if you must, but be aware that it is immeasurably improved by the addition of reconstituted dried mushrooms or fresh "wild" mushrooms. Remember, too, that although different types of mushrooms sport distinctive flavors and textures, most can be used interchangeably and can be combined. A dish that features oyster mushrooms, shiitakes, and the common button mushroom is more exciting than a dish containing one alone.

Makes 4 servings

Time: 30 minutes

2 ounces or more dried porcini mushrooms (optional; use if you have only button mushrooms for fresh)

2 tablespoons butter or extra-virgin olive oil

1 pound fresh mushrooms, preferably a combination of types, cleaned, trimmed, and sliced, the stems reserved for another use, a few slices reserved for garnish

Salt and freshly ground black pepper to taste

2 tablespoons minced shallots

1 teaspoon minced garlic

4 cups chicken, beef, or vegetable stock or store-bought broth, preferably warmed (you can use the microwave for this if it's easier)

Minced fresh parsley leaves for garnish

1 If you are using dried mushrooms, soak them in hot water to cover for about 15 minutes while you prepare the other ingredients.

2 Place the butter or oil in a large, deep saucepan or casserole and turn the heat to medium. When the butter melts or the oil is hot, add the fresh mushrooms and turn the heat to medium-high. Cook, stirring, for about 10 minutes, until they begin to brown. As they cook, drain the dried mushrooms if you're using them (strain and reserve their soaking liquid), and stir them into the mixture. Season the mushrooms with salt and pepper as they cook.

3 Add the shallots and garlic and cook, stirring, for 1 minute. Add the stock and reserved mushroom-soaking liquid and bring the mixture just about to a boil. (You may prepare the soup in advance up to this point. Cover, refrigerate for up to 2 days, and reheat before proceeding.) Turn off the heat, garnish, and serve.

Preparation Tips: Store fresh mushrooms, loosely wrapped in waxed paper (not plastic), in the refrigerator bin; they often keep upward of a week.

Rinse mushrooms as lightly as you can (they absorb water like a sponge if they sit in it), but make sure to get dirt out of hidden crevices; with some mushrooms, it's easier to trim them first. Cut off any hard or dried-out spots—usually just the end of the stem. The stems of most mushrooms are perfectly edible, but those of shiitake should be discarded or reserved for stock.

Cream of Mushroom Soup Reduce the amount of stock by 1 cup. Add 1 tablespoon dry sherry (optional) along with the stock. Stir in 1 cup light or heavy cream or half-and-half just before serving, and heat through (do not boil). Garnish with snipped chives and sliced mushrooms.

Kale and Potato Soup

Kale soup, a Portuguese specialty, is frequently spiced with sausage or thickened with cream. Here, however, its assertive flavor is complemented by marjoram, and pureed potato adds a pleasant texture without fat or meat.

Makes 4 servings

Time: 30 minutes

1 large baking potato, cut into eighths

1 clove garlic, lightly smashed

5 cups chicken, beef, or vegetable stock, store-bought broth, or water, preferably warmed

About 3 cups roughly chopped kale leaves and thin stems (well rinsed before chopping)

1 teaspoon fresh marjoram or oregano leaves or 1/2 teaspoon dried marjoram or oregano

1 bay leaf

Salt and freshly ground black pepper to taste

1   Combine the potato, garlic, and 2 cups of the stock or water in a medium saucepan and turn the heat to medium-high. Cook until the potato is soft, about 15 minutes; cool slightly. (You may prepare the soup in advance up to this point. Cover, refrigerate for up to 2 days, and reheat before proceeding.)

2   At the same time, cook the kale in the remaining stock or water with the marjoram and bay leaf until tender, about 10 minutes. Remove the bay leaf.

3   Puree the potato, garlic, and stock or water together; the mixture will be thick. Stir it into the simmering kale, season with salt and pepper, and heat through. Serve immediately.

Shopping Tip: Kale and collards—its flat-leaved relative—are interchangeable. Cooking time for either will be considerably shorter if you avoid thick stems; usually those with 1/4-inch-thick stems are easier to cook and to eat.

Kale and Potato Soup with Linguica   While the potato is cooking, slice about 1/2 pound of linguica (or kielbasa) into slices about 1/4-inch thick. Brown these quickly, on both sides, in a skillet, and add to the kale just before stirring in the potato-garlic mixture.

Preparing Kale and Collards

You may remove the stems if they are very thick (or simply cook them a little longer than the leaves). Cut on either side of them, at an angle.

The easiest way to chop large leaves is to roll them up and cut across the log from top to bottom.

Corn, Tomato, and Zucchini Soup with Basil

This is a fresh-tasting late-summer vegetable soup that should really be made only in season. If you don't have stock, follow the directions in Step 1 using water; the corncob stock will be sweet and delicious (use plenty of salt).

Makes 4 servings

Time: About 30 minutes

4 cups chicken or vegetable stock or store-bought broth

4 ears fresh corn

2 tablespoons butter or olive oil

1 medium onion, minced

2 cups cored, peeled, seeded, and chopped tomatoes, see illustration; canned are fine, drain them first

2 small or 1 medium zucchini, about ½ pound, diced

1 tablespoon minced garlic

Salt and freshly ground black pepper to taste

½ cup minced fresh basil leaves

1 teaspoon balsamic or other flavorful vinegar, or to taste

1 Heat the stock or broth in a large, deep saucepan. Strip the kernels from the corn (see illustration on page 98) and add the cobs to the stock (break them in half if necessary to fit them into the pot); let them simmer there while you prepare the other vegetables.

2 Place the butter or oil in a large, deep saucepan or casserole and turn the heat to medium. A minute later, add the onion and cook, stirring, until it begins to soften, about 5 minutes. Add the tomatoes, zucchini, garlic, salt, and pepper, and cook, stirring occasionally, for about 10 minutes.

3 Remove the corncobs from the stock and add the stock to the vegetables. Cook until the zucchini is tender but not mushy, about 5 minutes. Stir in the corn kernels and most of the basil. Add the vinegar. Taste and adjust seasoning as necessary.

4 Serve, garnishing with remaining basil.

Preparing Tomatoes

1	2	3	4

(**Step 1**) First, core the tomato. Cut a wedge right around the core and remove it. (**Step 2**) Then peel the tomato. Cut a small "x" in the flower (non-stem) end. Drop it into boiling water until the skin begins to loosen, usually less than thirty seconds. (**Step 3**) Remove the peels with a paring knife. (**Step 4**) Finish by seeding the tomato. The easiest way to remove seeds is to simply cut the tomato in half through its equator, then squeeze and shake out the seeds. Do this over a bowl if you wish to strain and reserve the juice.

Black Bean Soup

The best way to serve this soup with great Mexican flavors is to puree about half of it, then pour it back into the pot. But you can also just mash the contents of the pot with a potato masher or large fork to get a similar smooth-chunky effect.

Makes 4 to 6 servings

Time: 30 minutes with precooked beans

2 tablespoons canola or other neutral oil

2 medium onions, chopped

1 tablespoon minced garlic

1 tablespoon chili powder, or to taste

3 cups drained cooked or canned black beans

4 cups chicken, beef, or vegetable stock, store-bought broth, or water, preferably warmed

Salt and freshly ground black pepper to taste

2 teaspoons freshly squeezed lime juice, or to taste

Sour cream or plain yogurt for garnish

Minced cilantro leaves for garnish

1 Place the oil in a large, deep saucepan or casserole and turn the heat to medium. A minute later, add the onions and cook, stirring, until softened, about 5 minutes. Stir in the garlic and chili powder and cook, stirring, another minute.

2 Add the beans and stock or water and season with salt and pepper. Turn the heat to medium-high and bring the soup just about to a boil. Turn the heat to medium-low, and cook, stirring occasionally, for about 10 minutes. Turn off the heat.

3 Force half the contents of the pot through a food mill or carefully puree it in a food processor or blender; or just mash the contents with a potato masher or large fork. (You may prepare the soup in advance up to this point. Cover, refrigerate for up to 2 days, and reheat before proceeding.)

4 Add the lime juice and stir; taste and adjust seasonings as necessary. Serve, garnished with sour cream or yogurt and minced cilantro.

3 Quick Additions to Bean Soups

Bean soups are receptive to a wide variety of additions. Try:

1 Scraps of smoked meats, such as ham or bacon (or cook the beans with a ham bone)

2 Precooked vegetables like onions, carrots, or celery

3 Diced fresh tomatoes as a garnish

Quick Chicken Soup with Rice or Noodles

This is a thin chicken soup—a warming but not super-filling first course—with the rice, meat, and vegetables acting as a garnish rather than a major player; see the variation if you want something more substantial. Use orzo or other tiny pasta, angel hair or other thin noodles, ribbons or other egg noodles, or other cooked grains in place of the rice.

Makes 4 servings

Time: 30 minutes

5 to 6 cups chicken stock or store-bought broth

½ cup long-grain rice or pasta

1 carrot, peeled and cut into thin slices

1 celery stalk, minced (optional)

1 cup raw or cooked chopped boneless skinless chicken, or more

Salt and freshly ground black pepper to taste

Minced fresh parsley or dill leaves for garnish

1 Place the stock in a large, deep saucepan or casserole and turn the heat to medium-high. When it is just about boiling, turn the heat down to medium so that it bubbles but not too vigorously. Stir in the rice, carrot, and celery and cook, stirring occasionally, until they are all tender, about 20 minutes.

2 Stir in the chicken. If it is raw, cook another 5 to 8 minutes, until it is cooked. If it is cooked, cook 2 or 3 minutes, until it is hot. Season with salt and pepper, garnish, and serve.

Shopping Tip: Most canned broths are weak. Still, they're usually more flavorful than water (which is still a decent alternative). Generally, buy "low-sodium" varieties and avoid those containing MSG. Broths sold in boxes are a slightly better option because they don't have as much of the off flavors associated with canned foods.

Thick Chicken Soup with Rice or Noodles Increase the amount of rice or pasta to 1 cup; use 2 carrots and 2 celery stalks. Use as much chicken as you like. If you plan to store this soup, cook the rice separately and stir it in during the last stage of cooking or it will absorb too much liquid during storage.

Lightning-Quick Fish Soup

If you have fish stock and fish scraps in the freezer, combine them here. If not, use chicken stock or broth or water and fresh fish. I love a fish soup like this one with good, crusty bread, but you could also cook a few noodles (separately) and add them to the fish for a one-pot meal.

Makes 4 servings

Time: 20 minutes

5 cups fish, chicken, or shrimp stock, or water

1 large onion, chopped

1 tablespoon minced garlic

1 teaspoon paprika

Pinch saffron (optional)

1 tablespoon extra-virgin olive oil

1 cup cored, peeled, seeded, and chopped tomatoes (canned are fine; include their liquid)

Salt and freshly ground black pepper to taste

1½ pounds any white-fleshed fish, cut into small chunks, or fish mixed with shelled seafood, such as clams, shrimp, or scallops

Minced fresh parsley leaves for garnish

1   Combine all the ingredients except for the fish and parsley in a large, deep saucepan or casserole and turn the heat to high. Bring to a boil, then turn the heat to medium and cook for 5 minutes, stirring occasionally.

2   Add the fish and cook, stirring, until it cooks through, about 5 minutes. Garnish and serve.

Shopping Tip: If you're buying fish, especially for this or any other fish soup, look for sturdy, white-fleshed varieties like red snapper, monkfish, or grouper. Oily fish like salmon is too rich for soups, and delicate fish like flounder simply falls apart. Of course, shellfish—clams, mussels, shrimp, and so on—are perfect additions.

2 | Pasta

🌗 Pasta with Tomato Sauce   18

🌗 Pasta with Raw Tomato Sauce   19

Pasta with Broccoli   20

Ziti with Creamy Gorgonzola Sauce   21

Fettuccine with Spinach, Butter, and Cream   22

Penne with Ricotta, Parmesan, and Peas   23

Pasta with Onion and Bacon   24

Pasta with Sausage   26

Linguine with Scallops   27

Linguine with Clams   28

Cold Noodles with Sesame or Peanut Sauce   30

Crisp Pan-Fried Noodle Cake   31

🌗 20 minutes or less

Pasta with Tomato Sauce

Pasta with tomato sauce can't be beat for a quick, satisfying dish. And you can vary it in so many ways. You can pass freshly grated Parmesan (or Pecorino Romano) cheese with this, but it is not essential.

Makes about 4 servings

Time: 20 minutes

---

3 tablespoons olive oil

3 cloves garlic, lightly smashed, or
1 small onion, minced

1 (28-ounce) can whole plum tomatoes

Salt and freshly ground black pepper
to taste

1 pound linguine or other long pasta

---

3 Ways to Quickly Vary Tomato Sauce

1 Tomato Sauce with Herbs: Stir in 2 or 3 tablespoons of minced fresh basil leaves, or 1 teaspoon minced fresh oregano or marjoram leaves (or 1/2 teaspoon dried), while the tomatoes are cooking. Garnish with fresh minced parsley, basil, or mint leaves.

2 Puttanesca Sauce: Stir 2 tablespoons of capers (drained), some crushed red pepper flakes if you like, and/or 1/2 cup pitted black olives (the oil-cured type are best) into the sauce after adding the tomatoes.

3 Tuna Sauce: Add one (6-ounce) can tuna, preferably the Italian kind packed in olive oil, to the sauce after adding tomatoes. This is especially good with the additions given for Puttanesca, above.

1 Bring a large pot of water to a boil and salt it. Warm 2 tablespoons of the oil with the garlic or onion in a medium skillet over medium-low heat. Cook, stirring occasionally, until the garlic is lightly golden or the onion is translucent.

2 Drain the tomatoes and remove their seeds if you choose to do so. Crush them with a fork or your hands and add them to the skillet, along with salt and pepper. Raise the heat to medium-high and cook, stirring occasionally, until the tomatoes break down and the mixture becomes "saucy," about 10 minutes. Remove the garlic if you like. Stir in the remaining 1 tablespoon of oil, taste for salt, and add more if necessary. (This sauce may be covered and refrigerated for a day or two, or put in a closed container and frozen for several weeks.)

3 Meanwhile, cook the pasta until it is tender but not mushy. If necessary, ladle some of the cooking water into the sauce to thin it out a bit. Toss the pasta with the sauce and serve.

Cooking Tips: Long pastas, like spaghetti and linguine, are best with sauces that don't have large chunks in them. Chunky sauces are best served with bigger, tube-shaped pasta, such as penne, rigatoni, or ziti, or with shells and elbows (all of which gather in the chunks).

Don't change the type of sauce you're making because you don't have the "correct" pasta shape. If you make spaghetti with a chunky sauce, some of the sauce will stay at the bottom of the bowl. This is less than ideal, of course, but you can eat that sauce with a spoon, or some bread, and next time you shop you might remember to stock up on penne.

Pasta with Raw Tomato Sauce

This is pasta with a great fresh-tasting sauce, best made when tomatoes are worth eating. It's also a wonderful all-purpose topping that can be used as a dipping sauce for fried foods such as Sautéed Chicken Cutlets (page 52) or chips, for that matter. But do not use dried basil. And don't smash the garlic too roughly or you'll have trouble removing it before serving.

Makes about 4 servings

Time: About 20 minutes

2 cups cored and roughly chopped ripe tomatoes

2 tablespoons extra-virgin olive oil

Salt and freshly ground black pepper to taste

2 cloves garlic, smashed

¼ to ½ cup roughly minced fresh basil leaves

1 pound linguine or other long pasta

Freshly grated Parmesan cheese

1 Bring a large pot of water to a boil and salt it.

2 Place the tomatoes, oil, salt, pepper, garlic, and half the basil in a broad-bottomed bowl. Mash together well, using a fork or potato masher, but do not puree. (You can make the sauce an hour or two before you're ready to eat and let it rest, at room temperature.)

3 Cook the pasta until it is tender but not mushy. Ladle some of the cooking water into the sauce to thin it out a bit and warm it up. Remove the garlic. Toss the pasta with the sauce and top with the remaining basil; pass the grated Parmesan at the table.

Shopping Tip: The best quality pasta is made from 100% durum wheat. It is easier to keep from overcooking, has a deeper, more appealing color and a texture that "grabs" the sauce better. It may come from the United States, or from Italy—the difference in price can determine your preference, although Italian pasta is not expensive. Most experienced cooks choose Italian pasta, which is widely available.

Pasta with Broccoli

This is a big, flavorful, filling dish, which needs only bread to become a meal. For variety, substitute cauliflower, or broccoflower—a mild-flavored light green cauliflower look-alike, which will take about 10 minutes longer to cook.

Makes about 4 servings

Time: About 30 minutes

---

1 head broccoli, 1 pound or more

¼ cup olive oil

1 tablespoon minced garlic

1 pound penne, ziti, or other cut pasta

Salt and freshly ground black pepper to taste

Minced fresh parsley leaves for garnish

1 Bring a large pot of water to a boil and salt it.

2 Trim the broccoli and divide it into florets. Steam it over boiling water (in another pot) until it is tender but not soft when pierced by a knife (the broccoli will cook further in the sauce, so be careful not to overcook it), about 10 minutes. Remove the broccoli and set it aside.

3 Meanwhile, cook the oil and garlic together in a large, deep skillet over medium-low heat, stirring occasionally. When the garlic is golden, turn off the heat if you're not ready to proceed. Add the broccoli to the skillet and turn the heat to medium. Cook, stirring and mashing the broccoli, until it is hot and quite soft.

4 At the same time, cook the pasta in the large pot. When it is just about done, drain it, reserving about a cup of the cooking liquid. Add the pasta to the skillet with the broccoli and toss with a large spoon until well combined. Add salt and pepper, along with some of the pasta water to keep the mixture from drying out. Garnish and serve.

Ziti with Creamy Gorgonzola Sauce

The best Gorgonzola, which, not surprisingly, is imported from Italy, is soft and creamy to begin with. Combine it with butter and cream and you have luxury combined with intense flavor.

Makes about 4 servings

Time: 30 minutes

2 tablespoons butter

½ cup crumbled Gorgonzola cheese

½ cup milk, half-and-half, or cream

1 pound ziti, penne, or other cut pasta

½ cup freshly grated Parmesan cheese, plus more if desired

Salt to taste

1 Bring a large pot of water to a boil and salt it.

2 Melt the butter in a 1- or 2-quart saucepan over low heat. While it is melting, put the Gorgonzola in a small bowl and mash it with a fork or potato masher, gradually adding the milk. Don't worry about making it smooth, just make sure it is well combined. When the butter is melted, add the cheese-milk mixture and continue to cook, stirring and mashing occasionally.

3 Meanwhile, cook the pasta until it is tender but firm. When it is done, drain it and mix with the sauce in a large, warm bowl; stir in the Parmesan, then taste for salt and add some if necessary. Serve, passing additional Parmesan at the table if you like.

Shopping Tip: Use good-quality Gorgonzola or substitute another creamy blue cheese, such as Roquefort (from France—made from sheep's milk and especially delicious), or Stilton (from England). Try to avoid domestic blue cheeses, unless you can find a really special one, like Maytag blue.

Fettuccine with Spinach, Butter, and Cream

The combination of spinach and cream is old-fashioned but still wonderful. This sauce is also good with a tiny grating of nutmeg added to it.

Makes about 4 servings

Time: 30 minutes

10 ounces fresh spinach, trimmed, washed, and dried

4 tablespoons (1/2 stick) butter

Salt and freshly ground black pepper to taste

1/2 cup heavy cream, light cream, or half-and-half

1 pound spaghetti, linguine, or fettuccine

1 cup freshly grated Parmesan cheese

1   Bring a large pot of water to a boil and salt it.

2   Chop the spinach coarsely. Over medium heat melt 2 tablespoons of the butter in a large skillet that can later be covered. Add the spinach, along with some salt and pepper. Cover, reduce the heat, and cook, stirring occasionally, until the spinach is very tender, about 10 minutes. Uncover, add the cream, and cook gently for about 5 minutes.

3   Meanwhile, cook the pasta until it is tender but firm. When it is just about done, put the remaining butter in a large, warm bowl and add a couple of tablespoons of the cooking water. Drain the pasta and toss it with the butter and half the Parmesan. Add the spinach sauce and serve, passing the remaining Parmesan at the table.

Shopping Tip: Spinach leaves must be plump; any wilting or yellowing is a bad sign. Store it, loosely wrapped in plastic, in the vegetable bin, but use it as fast as you can. It will keep for a few days. Sold year-round, it's in season locally in cool but not cold or hot weather.

Preparation Tips: Wash spinach well, in several changes of water; it's sandy. Remove very thick stems, but leave thinner ones on; they'll be fine. Don't chop too finely before cooking, or you'll lose too many little pieces to the cooking liquid.

For a cooked dish like pasta with cream and spinach, frozen spinach is almost as good as fresh. Thaw it, squeeze out excess liquid, and proceed as in Step 2 (it's likely to have been chopped already).

Penne with Ricotta, Parmesan, and Peas

The butter is optional here, but it lends richness. Add a bit of minced sautéed ham or mushrooms if you like, or use basic tomato sauce (Pasta with Tomato Sauce, page 18) to thin the ricotta in place of the pasta cooking water.

Makes about 4 servings

Time: 30 minutes

1 cup freshly shelled or frozen peas

1 pound penne, ziti, or other cut pasta

About 1 cup fresh ricotta, available in Italian and specialty food markets

1 tablespoon softened butter (optional)

1 cup freshly grated Parmesan cheese

Salt and freshly ground black pepper to taste

1   Bring a large pot of water to a boil and salt it.

2   Cook the peas in boiling salted water to cover, just until tender, about 3 minutes. Drain and rinse in cold water to stop the cooking; drain and set aside.

3   Cook the pasta. While it is cooking, mix together the peas, ricotta, butter, and half of the Parmesan in the bottom of a warm bowl. When the pasta is just about done, remove about a cup of the pasta cooking water and use as much of it as you need to smooth the ricotta mixture into a sauce.

4   Toss the pasta with the ricotta mixture, add additional pasta cooking water if necessary, and serve, passing the remaining Parmesan at the table.

Shopping Tips: You cannot substitute for freshly grated cheese, and real Parmesan—among the world's greatest cheese from the area around Parma—is now sold everywhere. It can be expensive, but it lasts a long time (unless you start nibbling on it, which is understandable).

Look for the brown rind with "Parmigiano-Reggiano" stenciled on it. Everything else called "Parmesan" is an imitation, although some of the imitations (like Grana Padano) are decent; hard sheep's cheese ("pecorino Romano," for example) is stronger but a decent substitute on strong-flavored dishes.

Pasta with Onion and Bacon

This dish—called *linguine all'amatriciana*—is one of the greatest of all pasta dishes, sweet from onion, salty and meaty from pancetta or bacon, tart from tomatoes. The balance is incredible.

Makes about 4 servings

Time: 30 minutes

---

2 tablespoons olive oil

1/4 to 1/2 cup chopped pancetta or good bacon

1 small onion, diced

1 (28-ounce) can whole plum tomatoes, drained

1 pound linguine, spaghetti, fettuccine, or other long pasta

Salt and freshly ground black pepper to taste

Freshly grated Parmesan or pecorino Romano cheese

Minced fresh parsley leaves

1 Bring a large pot of water to a boil and salt it.

2 Place the oil and pancetta or bacon in a medium skillet over medium heat. Cook, stirring, until the meat becomes crisp, about 10 minutes.

3 When the meat is done, remove it with a slotted spoon, leaving the fat in the pan. Add the onion and cook, stirring, until it browns. Turn off the heat for a minute (this will reduce the spattering when you add the tomatoes).

4 Crush the tomatoes with a fork or your hands and add them to the pan. Turn the heat to medium-high. Cook, stirring occasionally, until the tomatoes break down and the mixture becomes saucy, about 10 to 15 minutes.

5 Meanwhile, cook the pasta until it is tender but not mushy. Drain it, toss it with the sauce, and top with the reserved bacon, the Parmesan, and the parsley. Serve, passing additional Parmesan at the table.

Shopping Tip: Pancetta is cured—that is, salted—unsmoked bacon. It's available at good Italian markets. Buy 1/4-inch-thick slices, and freeze them individually; you don't even have to thaw them before using in recipes like this one.

Preparing Onions

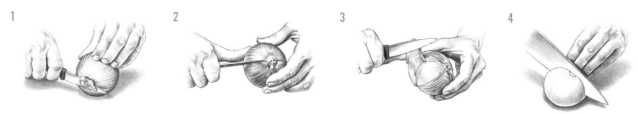

(Step 1) Cut off both ends of the onion. **(Steps 2–3)** Then make a small slit in the skin, just one layer down. The peel will come off easily. **(Step 4)** Cut the onion in half.

(Step 5) Make two or three cuts parallel to the cutting board into the vegetable; don't cut all the way through. **(Step 6)** Now make several cuts down through the top of the vegetable. Again leave the vegetable intact at one end. **(Step 7)** Cut across the vegetable to create a dice.

Pasta with Sausage

Removing the sausage from its casing leaves you with deliciously chewy and spicy bits of sausage. Do not brown the sausage, in the pan; it should just cook through. Serve this hearty dish with a vegetable side dish such as simple Buttered Peas (page 101) or Chard with Pine Nuts and Currants (page 97).

Makes 4 to 6 servings

Time: 30 minutes or less

Salt and freshly ground black pepper

1 tablespoon butter

1/2 pound sweet or hot Italian sausage, removed from the casing if necessary

1/2 cup water

1 pound ziti or other cut pasta

1/2 cup or more freshly grated Parmesan cheese

1 Bring a large pot of water to a boil for the pasta and salt it.

2 Place the butter in a medium skillet over medium-low heat. As it melts, crumble the sausage meat into it, making the bits quite small, 1/2 inch or less in size. Add the water and adjust the heat so that the mixture simmers gently.

3 Cook the pasta until it is tender but not mushy. Reserve about 1/2 cup of the pasta-cooking water.

4 Drain the pasta and dress with the sauce, adding some of the reserved cooking liquid if necessary. Taste and add salt and pepper as necessary. Toss with the Parmesan and serve.

Shopping Tip: For this recipe, you want Italian sausage, preferably freshly made in patties (most Italian markets have this, as do some supermarkets). If that's unavailable, use links of Italian sausage—hot or sweet—but remove the meat from its casing. Some of the new varieties of sausage, including those made from chicken or turkey, can be quite good, but those labeled "low-fat" are often "low-flavor," too.

Linguine with Scallops

You can use this recipe for sea, bay, or calico scallops. Take care to keep the cooking time brief, not only to avoid over-cooking but to preserve the liquid given up by the scallops.

Makes about 4 servings

Time: 30 minutes

¾ pound sea, bay, or calico scallops

¼ cup olive oil, plus 1 tablespoon

4 tablespoons (½ stick) butter (optional)

1 tablespoon minced garlic

Salt and freshly ground black pepper to taste

¼ cup toasted plain bread crumbs

½ cup minced fresh parsley leaves

1 pound linguine or spaghetti

1 Bring a large pot of water to a boil and salt it. If you're using sea scallops, cut them into ¼- to ½-inch chunks; cut bay scallops in half; leave calicos whole.

2 Combine the ¼ cup olive oil with the butter, if you are using it, and the garlic in a small saucepan over low heat. Cook until the garlic turns pale tan, stirring occasionally. Raise the heat to medium-high, add the scallops, salt, and pepper, and cook just until the surface of the scallops turns opaque, about 2 minutes. Add the bread crumbs and half the parsley and turn off the heat.

3 Cook the pasta until it is tender but not mushy. When it is just about done, reheat the scallops over medium heat. Drain the pasta, reserving some of the cooking liquid if you omitted the butter. Toss the pasta with the sauce and the remaining olive oil, add a little pasta-cooking water if necessary, and top with the remaining parsley.

Shopping Tips: The best scallops are either bay scallops (when available) or sea scallops. The least desirable (and of course the least expensive) are the tiny calicos, not much bigger than pencil erasers and just as rubbery when overcooked.

Many scallops are soaked in phosphates, which cause them to absorb water and lose flavor. Always buy scallops from someone you trust, and let him or her know that you want unsoaked (sometimes called "dry") scallops.

Linguine with Clams

This is not only a terrific pasta recipe, but the most basic and essential way to prepare clams. If you are using littlenecks or other hardshell clams, steam them exactly as they're done here; you'll want at least a dozen medium or two dozen small clams per person, even as an appetizer. If you are using "steamers"—softshell clams—follow the same procedure, but serve a cup of the steaming liquid alongside the clams to rinse the meat after it's been removed from the shell: it is invariably sandy.

Makes about 4 servings

Time: 30 minutes

At least 40 littleneck clams, the smaller the better, or at least 3 pounds of cockles

½ cup dry white wine, plus little more if necessary

Pinch of cayenne

¼ cup extra-virgin olive oil

1 tablespoon minced garlic

Salt

1 pound long pasta, such as linguine or spaghetti

1 large or 2 small plum tomatoes, peeled, seeded, and minced (optional)

½ teaspoon minced fresh tarragon, or 1 tablespoon minced fresh basil or chervil

¾ cup roughly chopped parsley

1 Bring a large pot of water to a boil and salt it.

2 Wash the clams well, scrubbing them with a soft brush if necessary. Place them in a broad saucepan or skillet with a cover, along with the wine and cayenne. Cover and turn the heat to high. Cook, shaking the pan occasionally. After 3 minutes, check the clams to see if any have opened. As soon as the majority of littlenecks or cockles are open, remove them; don't worry if many are still closed. Transfer the clams to a bowl. Pass the juice through a sieve lined with cheesecloth to remove all traces of sand.

3 Combine the olive oil and minced garlic in a broad, deep skillet and turn the heat to medium. When the garlic starts to sizzle, begin cooking the pasta; you will want it to be quite firm when it's done. Turn the heat under the garlic to low and cook, shaking the pan occasionally, just until the garlic begins to color, about 5 minutes.

4 Measure the clam juice; if it is less than a cup, add the tomatoes, or as much wine as you would need to make a cup of juice to the garlic in the skillet (do not add the clam juice yet). You can add the tomatoes if you like, but do not add additional wine if you have a cup of clam juice. Raise the heat to high and let the mixture bubble for about 2 minutes; stir in the tarragon.

5 Stir in the clams and cover; cook over high heat until almost all of the clams open, another minute or two. (Don't worry if some of the clams never open, as often happens with littlenecks; just open them with a paring or similar knife.) Drain the pasta and toss it into the skillet with the clams; add the reserved clam juice and cook for 30 seconds, or until the pasta is tender but still firm and the sauce is a pleasing consistency. Stir in the parsley and serve.

Shopping Tips: The biggest and toughest clams are chopped into bits to be made into chowder. The choicest—essentially the smallest—are sold live, and are great raw, on the half-shell. In recent years we have seen more and more cockles—very small clams—in our markets, and they are the best for this recipe.

Buying clams is easy, because those in the shell must be alive. You'd know when hard-shells have died; the shells separate easily. Otherwise, they're shut up pretty tight, and you cannot even slide their shells from side to side. Dead clams smell pretty bad, so it's unlikely you'll be fooled.

Preparation Tips: Never store clams in sealed plastic or under water; they'll die. Just keep them in a bowl in the refrigerator, where they will remain alive for several days.

Hard-shell clams require little more than a cleaning of their shells. I use a stiff brush to scrub them under running water.

Cold Noodles with Sesame or Peanut Sauce

A wonderful starter or side dish; the noodles and sauce each can be made in advance and combined at the last minute. Add cooked shredded chicken and seeded and diced cucumber to this for substance and crunch. (If you have extra time, after tossing the noodles with the sesame oil, refrigerate the noodles for up to 2 hours for best flavor.)

Makes 4 to 6 servings

Time: About 30 minutes

12 ounces fresh egg noodles, or any dried noodles, such as spaghetti

2 tablespoons dark sesame oil

1/2 cup sesame paste (tahini) or natural peanut butter

1 tablespoon sugar

1/4 cup soy sauce

1 tablespoon rice or wine vinegar

Hot sesame oil, chili-garlic sauce, Tabasco, or other hot sauce to taste

Salt and freshly ground black pepper to taste

At least 1/2 cup minced scallions for garnish

1 Cook the noodles in boiling salted water until tender but not mushy. Drain, then rinse in cold water for a minute or two. Toss with half the sesame oil.

2 Beat together the tahini or peanut butter, sugar, soy sauce, and vinegar. Add a little hot sauce and salt and pepper; taste and adjust seasoning as necessary. Thin the sauce with hot water, so that it is about the consistency of heavy cream.

3 Toss together the noodles and the sauce, and add more of any seasoning if necessary. Drizzle with the remaining sesame oil, garnish, and serve.

Crisp Pan-Fried Noodle Cake

A great side dish for almost any meal that has some spice, Chinese or not, this noodle cake is most appropriately used in place of rice as a bed for any moist stir-fry, such as Stir-Fried Chicken with Broccoli or Cauliflower (page 58). Great hot or at room temperature as a snack, too.

Makes 4 to 6 servings

Time: 30 minutes

12 ounces fresh egg noodles

1/4 cup minced scallion

1 tablespoon soy sauce

4 tablespoons peanut (preferred) or other oil, plus more if needed

1 Cook the noodles in boiling salted water until tender but not mushy. Drain, then rinse in cold water for a minute or two. Toss with the scallion, soy sauce, and 1 tablespoon of the oil.

2 Place the remaining oil on the bottom of a heavy medium to large skillet, preferably non-stick; turn the heat to medium-high. When the oil is hot, add the noodle mix, spreading it out evenly and pressing it down.

3 Cook 2 minutes, then turn the heat to medium-low. Continue to cook until the cake is holding together and is nicely browned on the bottom. Turn carefully (the easiest way to do this is to slide the cake out onto a plate, cover it with another plate, invert the plates, and slide the cake back into the skillet, browned side up), adding a little more oil if necessary.

4 Cook on the other side until brown, then cut into pie-like wedges, and serve.

3 | Fish

Broiled Flatfish or Other Thin White Fillets   34

Sautéed Flatfish or Other Thin White Fillets   36

Sautéed Cod or Other Thick White Fillets   38

Red Snapper or Other Fillets in Packages with Spinach   39

Grilled Mesclun-Stuffed Tuna or Swordfish Steaks   40

Poached Halibut or Other Fish Steaks with Vegetables   41

Salmon Roasted in Butter   42

Broiled Shrimp, My Way   43

Shrimp "Marinara"   44

Roast Shrimp with Tomatoes   45

Sautéed Scallops   46

Warm Salad of Scallops and Tender Greens   47

20 minutes or less

Broiled Flatfish or Other Thin White Fillets

Simpler and faster than a steak—or almost anything else. As always with fresh fish, it must smell of seawater, no more; that's the best indicator of quality.

Makes 4 servings

Time: 15 minutes

About 1½ pounds fillets of flounder, sole, or any of the other fish listed on page 37, cut about ¼ inch thick, scaled or skinned

1 tablespoon olive oil or melted butter, plus a little more for the pan

Salt and freshly ground black pepper to taste

Lemon quarters or a sprinkling of vinegar

1 Preheat the broiler. It should be very hot, and the rack should be as close to the heat source as you can get it—even 2 inches is not too close. (You can also bake the fish at 450°F; it will take a minute or two longer.)

2 Lightly grease a baking sheet or broiling pan. Lay the fillets on it, then brush with the tablespoon of oil or butter. Sprinkle with salt and pepper.

3 Broil the fish for 2 to 4 minutes (without turning), depending on the heat of your oven and the distance from the heat source. (If the fish is thicker than ¼ inch, adjust cooking time accordingly, but few of these fillets will take more than 5 minutes in most ovens.) When the fish is done, it should be firm and barely cooked through; the edges will flake, but the center should still show a little resistance. If there is a little translucence in the very middle, it will disappear by the time you get the fish onto a plate.

4 Remove the fish with a spatula and serve immediately, squeezing lemon juice or drizzling vinegar over the fillets at the table. Serve immediately.

Cooking Tip: Thin fish fillets cook very, very quickly and overcook almost as fast. A ¼-inch-thick flounder fillet can, under the right circumstances, cook through in 2 minutes. Even a relatively thick piece of red snapper will be done in less than 10 minutes in almost every instance.

Broiled Flatfish or Other Thin White Fillets with Mustard and Herbs Steps 1 and 2 remain the same. Combine 1/3 cup Dijon mustard, 1 tablespoon sugar, 1 teaspoon minced fresh thyme leaves or 1/2 teaspoon dried thyme (or substitute rosemary or savory; or parsley, chervil, or basil in larger quantities) and 1 tablespoon freshly squeezed lemon juice. Spread this mixture over the fish. Proceed with Steps 3 and 4 as above; serve with lemon wedges.

Broiled Flatfish or Other Thin White Fillets with Garlic-Parsley Sauce Steps 1 and 2 remain the same; use olive oil. Combine 1 teaspoon minced garlic, 1/3 cup extra-virgin olive oil, 1/4 cup freshly squeezed lemon juice, 1/2 cup minced fresh parsley leaves, and a little salt and pepper. Spoon some of this mixture over the fish. Proceed with Steps 3 and 4 as above; pass the rest of the sauce at the table.

4 Quick Ideas for Broiled Fillets

1 Brush lightly, before and after cooking, with butter, oil, or Vinaigrette (page 3)

2 Broil plain, as in the master recipe, and serve with your favorite salsa

3 Serve over a bed of lightly dressed salad greens

4 Use cold or hot in sandwiches, with mayonnaise or other dressing

Sautéed Flatfish or Other Thin White Fillets

This classic dish made with a simple butter sauce—called *sole meunière*—works equally well for any thin flatfish fillets. Note that this is for two people; if there is a disadvantage to this recipe, it is that the thinness of the fillets makes pan-cooking difficult—they simply take up too much room. Cook in batches if you're going to double the recipe. And serve the fish hot, hot, hot.

Makes 2 servings

Time: 20 minutes

About ½ to ¾ pound fillets of sole, flounder, or other fish listed at right, cut about ¼ inch thick, scaled or skinned

Salt and freshly ground black pepper to taste

1 tablespoon extra-virgin olive oil

4 tablespoons (½ stick) butter

Flour for dredging

2 tablespoons freshly squeezed lemon juice

Minced fresh parsley leaves for garnish

Lemon wedges

1   Heat two dinner plates in a 200°F oven. Season the fillets with salt and pepper.

2   Heat a large skillet, preferably non-stick, over medium-high heat for 2 or 3 minutes. Add the oil and half the butter. When the butter foam subsides, dredge the fillets, one by one, in the flour, shaking off any excess, and add them to the pan. Raise the heat to high and cook the fillets until golden on each side, 4 to 5 minutes total. Remove to the warm serving plates.

3   Turn the heat to medium and add the remaining butter to the pan. Cook until the butter foams, a minute or two. Add the lemon juice, and cook, stirring and scraping the bottom of the pan, for about 15 seconds. Pour the sauce over the fillets.

4   Garnish and serve immediately with the lemon wedges.

Preparation Tip: I usually don't bother to heat plates, but thin fish fillets cool off so quickly that it's worth it in this instance. If you don't want to turn on the oven, run the plates under steaming hot water for a minute, then dry.

Cooking Tip: If you use a non-stick skillet, you can turn a fish fillet—even one cooked in a minimum of fat—without much trouble. Make sure to turn it before it is fully cooked, however, or it may fall apart. Try turning after just 2 minutes of cooking.

◐ Sautéed Flatfish or Other Thin White Fillets with Curry and Lime Same technique, markedly different results. First, rub the fish with 1 tablespoon freshly squeezed lime juice. Mix together 1 teaspoon salt, 1/2 teaspoon ground black pepper, and 1 tablespoon curry powder or similar spice mixture. Rub this into the fish. Proceed with Steps 1 and 2, using no butter and just enough peanut or vegetable oil to cook the fish. Use 3 tablespoons of lime juice in Step 3, minced cilantro and lime wedges in Step 4.

◐ Sautéed Flatfish or Other Thin White Fillets with Soy Sauce Steps 1 and 2 remain the same; use peanut or vegetable oil in place of the butter. In Step 3, add an additional tablespoon of oil to the pan and, over medium heat, add 1 teaspoon minced garlic, 1 tablespoon peeled and minced or grated fresh ginger, and 2 minced scallions; cook, stirring, about 30 seconds. Add 1/2 cup any broth, white wine, or water, and let it bubble away for 30 seconds or so. Add 2 tablespoons soy sauce and the juice of 1 lime. Pour this sauce over the fish. Serve with lime wedges.

◐ Sautéed Flatfish or Other Thin White Fillets with Sesame Crust Very crisp and tasty. First, rub the fish with 1 tablespoon dark sesame oil. Proceed with Step 1. In Step 2, dredge the fillets in 1 cup toasted sesame seeds instead of flour, patting to make the seeds adhere; use peanut or vegetable oil in place of the butter. No additional liquid is needed in cooking. Serve with a dipping sauce of 3 tablespoons soy sauce, 1 tablespoon white or rice vinegar, 1 teaspoon dark sesame oil, and a dash of cayenne (optional).

Common Thin White Fish Fillets

A wide variety of thin fillets can be used for many recipes, as long as they are well under an inch thick. A ◆ indicates the sturdier fillets. Look for:

◆ Catfish

Flatfish of any type: Flounder, Fluke, Sole, Dab, Plaice

Haddock (likely to have skin on, but skin is edible)

Large- or Small-Mouthed Bass (freshwater)

Pickerel or Pike (freshwater)

Ocean Perch

◆ Red Snapper, or other Snappers

◆ Rockfish of any type

◆ Sea Bass

Whiting, also known as Hake

Sautéed Cod or Other Thick White Fillets

Take a fresh thick white fillet and cook it so that it's crisp on the outside and still tender and moist on the inside. Douse it with freshly squeezed lemon juice and you have one of eating's great pleasures.

Makes 4 servings

Time: 20 minutes

¼ cup olive, peanut, or vegetable oil

Salt and freshly ground black pepper to taste

2 cod fillets, or any of the fish listed below, about 1½ pounds (or 1 fillet cut into 2 or 4 pieces)

Flour for dredging

Minced fresh parsley leaves for garnish (optional)

Lemon wedges

Thick White Fish Fillets

There are many thick white fillets, which can be used for broiling, roasting, and sautéeing. A ◆ indicates the firmest fillets. Look for:

◆ Blackfish

  Cod

◆ Grouper

◆ Monkfish

  Orange Roughy

  Pacific Pollock, also known as Alaskan Pollock

  Red Snapper, or other Snappers

◆ Striped Bass

  Tilefish

  Whiting, also known as Hake

1 Heat a large skillet, preferably non-stick, over medium-high heat for 2 or 3 minutes. Add the oil to the skillet and, when it is hot (a pinch of flour will sizzle), season the fillets well, then dredge them in the flour, shaking off any excess. Add them to the pan.

2 Raise the heat to high and cook until browned on each side, turning once. Total cooking time will be about 10 minutes. Any thick fillet, when done, will still be firm and juicy, but will have lost its translucence, and a thin-bladed knife will pass through it fairly easily. The sturdier fillets (those marked with a ◆ at left) will take a minute or two longer than cod and other relatively delicate fish.

3 Garnish and serve with lemon wedges.

Shopping Tip: Some of the thick fillet choices are from the same fish as some thin fillets (they're simply cut from larger fish), and some from fish that produce only thick fillets. In any case, they're all white, tender, and mild-flavored, at least an inch thick (and usually considerably thicker than that—1½ inches is common, and 2 inches not unheard of).

Extra-Crisp Sautéed Cod or Other Thick White Fillets In Step 1, dip the fillet in the flour, shake off the excess, then dip in a bowl containing 2 beaten eggs. Dip in flour again, or in plain bread crumbs. Steps 2 and 3 remain the same.

Red Snapper or Other Fillets in Packages with Spinach

Cooking in packages—or *en papillote*—is fun and virtually foolproof. Since all of the fish's essences are locked within the foil or parchment package, moistness is guaranteed. But because you can't peek into the packages to judge doneness, I wouldn't make this with very thin fillets, which are likely to overcook. On the other hand, it's a fine recipe for some of the thicker fillets detailed at left.

Makes 4 servings

Time: 30 minutes

10 ounces spinach, tough stems removed, well washed, and roughly chopped

4 red snapper fillets or other thick fillets from page 38, 4 to 6 ounces each, scaled or skinned

¼ cup chopped sun-dried tomatoes

Salt and freshly ground black pepper to taste

4 sprigs tarragon

About 2 tablespoons olive oil

1 Preheat the oven to 450°F. Cut six 18-inch squares of aluminum foil or parchment paper then fold in half to make a double layer. On the bottom of each foil piece, place about ¼ of the spinach, then spread it over an area roughly the same size as the fillet; top with a piece of fish, about 1 tablespoon sun-dried tomatoes, salt, pepper, a sprig of tarragon, and a drizzle of oil. Fold the foil over the fish to cover, crimp the edges all the way around to seal the packages, and place the packages in a single layer in a large baking dish.

2 Bake for about 20 to 25 minutes, turning the pan in the oven after 10 minutes to ensure even cooking. Check the fish in one package; the snapper will be white, opaque, and tender when done, the tomato will have liquefied, and the spinach will be wilted and tender. Serve the packages closed, allowing each diner to open his or her own at the table.

Cooking Tip: Fresh tarragon is delicious, but it's also one of the few herbs that dries well. Use just a pinch of dried tarragon, crumbled between your fingers, in place of a sprig. Other herbs that are good in this dish are fresh thyme (again, a sprig, or use a pinch of dried), or fresh basil (a few leaves per fish package), parsley (a sprig or two per package), or chervil (again, a sprig or two per package)—the dried versions of these herbs are useless.

Grilled Mesclun-Stuffed Tuna or Swordfish Steaks

Preheat the grill while you prepare the fish, and this glorious dish can be completed in about a half hour. Do not be intimidated by the creation of the pocket; it is easy, and takes just a minute.

Makes 4 servings

Time: About 30 minutes

Juice of 2 limes

1/4 cup soy sauce

1 medium clove garlic, minced

1 teaspoon strong mustard

2 teaspoons peeled and finely minced fresh ginger or 1 teaspoon ground ginger

1/2 teaspoon dark sesame oil

1/2 teaspoon coarsely ground black pepper

1/4 cup dry white wine or water

1 tuna or swordfish steak, no less than 1 1/4 inches thick, about 1 1/2 pounds

About 1 1/2 cups mesclun or other assorted greens (trimmed, washed, dried, and torn)

1 Start a charcoal or wood fire or preheat a gas grill or broiler; the rack should be 3 to 4 inches from the heat source. Mix together all the ingredients except the tuna and the greens.

2 Using a sharp, thin-bladed knife (a boning knife, for example), make a small incision halfway down any edge of the tuna steak. Insert the knife almost to the opposite edge of the steak, then move it back and forth, flipping it over and creating a large pocket. Be careful not to cut through the top, bottom, or opposite edge of the tuna. Put the tuna in the soy mixture; you can leave it there for a few minutes or continue with the recipe right away.

3 Remove the tuna from the liquid and dry it with paper towels. Toss the mesclun with the marinade. Stuff the pocket with the mesclun, still drenched in the liquid. Seal the pocket opening with a couple of toothpicks.

4 Grill the tuna, turning once, about 5 minutes per inch of thickness (if your steak is 1 1/2 inches thick, for example, turn it after about 4 minutes and cook 3 or 4 minutes more). It will be quite rare; if you want to cook it more, go right ahead. Serve cut into quarters or 1/2-inch-thick slices.

Shopping Tip: Dark sesame oil, sold in almost every Asian market and many supermarkets, is roasted, and completely different from ordinary "light" sesame oil, which is a simple, almost tasteless, cooking oil. Store dark sesame oil in the refrigerator, and use it for dressings like this one, or at the end of stir-fries.

Poached Halibut or Other Fish Steaks with Vegetables

You can use this recipe and its variations for any fish steak (or sturdy fillet, for that matter), but I think it's best with mild-flavored ones—not only halibut, but cod, grouper, monkfish, and tilefish.

Makes 4 servings

Time: 30 minutes

About 2 cups any fish, chicken, or mild vegetable stock or store-bought broth

3 tablespoons butter

2 medium carrots, peeled and diced

2 medium onions, diced

2 stalks celery, diced

1 clove garlic, minced

Salt and freshly ground black pepper to taste

2 halibut steaks (or see headnote), ¾ to 1 pound each

1 In a small saucepan, bring the stock to a boil. Lower the heat, and keep it warm.

2 In the smallest skillet or casserole that will later hold the fish steaks, melt the butter over medium heat. Add all ingredients except fish and stock and cook, stirring, until the vegetables wilt, 5 to 10 minutes.

3 Place the steaks on top of the vegetables and add the stock. Simmer over medium-low heat until the halibut is done, about 10 minutes (a thin-bladed knife inserted between bone and flesh should reveal little or no translucence). Remove the steaks, cut each in half, and serve, topped with vegetables and a little of the broth.

Poached Halibut or Other Steaks with Vegetables and Mustard Sauce Steps 1 through 3 remain the same, but undercook the fish slightly, remove it and the vegetables from the pan, and keep them all warm in a warm oven. Melt 1 tablespoon butter in a small saucepan over medium-low heat. Add 1 table-spoon flour and cook, stirring, until the mixture turns nut-brown, about 3 or 4 minutes. Strain 1 cup of the fish-cooking liquid and whisk it gradually into the butter-flour mixture, stirring constantly to eliminate lumps. Cook until slightly thickened, 4 or 5 minutes. Season with salt and pepper and add 1 to 2 tablespoons Dijon mustard, or to taste. Serve the halibut and vegetables topped with the sauce and minced fresh parsley leaves.

Salmon Roasted in Butter

If you make this with the most flavorful, beautiful fillet you can find—such as Alaskan sockeye (its season is summer), or a lovely side of farm-raised salmon—you will be amazed by the richness of flavor.

Makes 4 to 8 servings

Time: 15 minutes

4 tablespoons (½ stick) butter

1 (2- to 3-pound) salmon fillet, skin on (but scaled) or off, pin bones removed

Salt and freshly ground black pepper to taste

Minced fresh parsley leaves for garnish

Removing Pin Bones

1

2

(Step 1) Fillets of many fish, no matter how skillfully removed, may contain long bones along their center which must be removed by hand. Feel with your fingers to see if your fillet contains pin bones. **(Step 2)** Remove them with needle-nose pliers or similar tool.

1 Preheat the oven to 475°F. Melt the butter in a medium roasting pan—either on top of the stove or in the oven as it preheats—until the foam subsides.

2 Place the salmon in the butter, flesh side down, and put the pan in the oven. Roast about 5 minutes, then turn and roast 3 to 6 minutes longer, until the salmon is done (peek between the flakes with a thin-bladed knife). Sprinkle with salt and pepper, garnish, and serve immediately.

Shopping Tip: Farm-raised salmon ("Norwegian salmon," a widely used misnomer) is available year-round and is fairly flavorful and usually inexpensive. Wild salmon, from the Pacific Northwest, is only available fresh from spring to fall, but it's preferable, especially if you can find king (chinook), sockeye (red), or coho (silver). Chum and pink salmon are less valued but still good wild varieties.

Cooking Tip: The cooking time for salmon varies according to your taste. I prefer my salmon cooked to what might be called medium-rare to medium, with a well-cooked exterior and a fairly red center. So, I always look at the center of a piece of salmon to judge its doneness. Remember that fish retains enough heat to continue cooking after it has been removed from the heat source, so stop cooking just before the salmon reaches the point you'd consider it done.

Salmon Roasted with Herbs This lower-fat version is equally flavorful. In Step 1, use 2 tablespoons olive oil, or half oil and half butter. In Step 2, add a handful (2 to 4 tablespoons depending on their strength) of chopped fresh herbs: tarragon, parsley, chervil, basil, dill, thyme, or a combination, and 2 tablespoons minced shallots, then roast as above.

Salmon Roasted with Buttered Almonds In Step 1, use only 1 tablespoon of oil or butter. Before cooking the fish, melt 3 tablespoons of butter in a small saucepan over medium-low heat. When the butter foam subsides, add 1 cup blanched slivered almonds and cook, stirring, just until they begin to brown. Place the fish in the pan, season with salt and pepper, and spoon the browned almonds on top. Roast as in Step 2, but without turning.

Broiled Shrimp, My Way

This recipe is so good it makes people go nuts; if you like scampi, try this (or the scampi variation). It pays to look for good, fresh paprika for this recipe; if you have a can or jar that's been open for two years, think about buying a new one.

Makes 4 servings

Time: About 30 minutes

½ cup extra-virgin olive oil

3 or 4 big cloves garlic, cut into slivers

1½ to 2 pounds shrimp, in the 20 to 30 per pound range, peeled, rinsed, and dried

Salt and freshly ground black pepper to taste

1 teaspoon ground cumin

1½ teaspoons fresh spicy paprika

Minced fresh parsley leaves for garnish

Preparing Shrimp

1

2

(Step 1) To peel shrimp, grasp the feelers on the underside and pull the peel away from the meat. (Step 2) To devein, make a shallow cut on the back of each shrimp, then pull out the long, black, threadlike vein.

1. Preheat the broiler and adjust the rack so that it is as close to the heat source as possible.

2. Very gently, in a large, broad ovenproof skillet or baking pan, warm the olive oil over low heat. There should be enough olive oil to cover the bottom of the pan; don't skimp. Put the garlic in the oil and cook for a few minutes, still over low heat, until it turns golden.

3. Raise the heat to medium-high and add the shrimp, salt, pepper, cumin, and paprika. Stir to blend and immediately place under the broiler. Cook, shaking the pan once or twice and stirring if necessary, but generally leaving the shrimp undisturbed, until they are pink all over and the mixture is bubbly. This will take from 5 to 10 minutes, depending on the heat of your broiler. Garnish and serve immediately.

Shrimp "Scampi" Don't preheat the broiler; use a large, deep skillet instead. Step 2 remains the same. In Step 3, omit the cumin and paprika. When the shrimp turns pink on one side, turn it over and add ¼ cup minced fresh parsley leaves. Raise the heat slightly and cook until the shrimp are done, about 2 minutes more. Stir in 1 tablespoon freshly squeezed lemon juice, dry sherry, vinegar, or white wine if you like and cook another 30 seconds before garnishing with more parsley and serving.

Shrimp with Spicy Orange Flavor Follow the directions for the Shrimp "Scampi" variation. Add 2 or more small dried hot red chiles and the roughly chopped peel of 1 orange along with the garlic. Add the juice of the orange along with the shrimp and spices. Substitute cilantro for the parsley if you like.

Shrimp "Marinara"

A tried-and-true dish, still a favorite in old-style Italian restaurants throughout the country and could be in your house. With fresh herbs, it's a revelation. Make plain white rice or pasta while you prepare this dish.

Makes 4 servings

Time: 20 minutes

2 tablespoons olive oil

1 tablespoon minced garlic

4 cups cored and chopped canned or fresh tomatoes, with their liquid

1/2 cup chopped fresh basil leaves

1 teaspoon minced fresh oregano or marjoram leaves or 1/4 teaspoon dried oregano or marjoram

1/2 teaspoon freshly ground black pepper

Salt to taste

1 pound shrimp, in the 20 to 30 per pound range, peeled, rinsed, and dried

1 Heat the oil over medium-low heat for 1 minute. Add the garlic and cook, stirring once or twice, until golden, 3 or 4 minutes.

2 Add the tomatoes, raise the heat to medium-high, and let bubble, stirring occasionally, for about 10 minutes. Add half the basil, the oregano, pepper, and salt. Stir and taste for seasoning. Reduce the heat to medium and let simmer while you cook rice or pasta if you choose to do so.

3 When you're just about ready to eat, add the shrimp to the sauce; cook until the shrimp are firm and pink, about 5 minutes. Remove 3 or 4 shrimp from the sauce and set aside. Toss the sauce with pasta, or spoon it over rice; top with the remaining basil and the reserved shrimp, and serve.

Shrimp with Feta Cheese This is better over rice than noodles. Step 1 remains the same. In Step 2, use 1 1/2 cups tomatoes and 1/2 cup dry white wine; omit the basil and use 2 tablespoons of minced fresh parsley leaves. Be careful in adding salt, because the feta cheese is quite salty. When the shrimp are done in Step 3, gently stir in 4 ounces of fresh feta cheese, cut into 1/2-inch cubes. Garnish with a little more parsley and serve immediately.

Roast Shrimp with Tomatoes

If you have nice, juicy tomatoes to moisten the bread crumbs, stick to these proportions. If your tomatoes are dry, cut back on the bread crumbs or increase the butter a little.

Makes 4 servings

Time: 30 minutes

4 tablespoons (½ stick) butter, more or less, or use extra-virgin olive oil

¾ cup plain bread crumbs, preferably fresh

½ cup minced fresh parsley leaves

1 teaspoon minced garlic

Salt and freshly ground black pepper to taste

1½ to 2 pounds shrimp, in the 20 to 30 per pound range, peeled, rinsed, and dried

About 12 thick slices ripe tomato

1 Preheat the oven to 450°F. Melt about half the butter over medium heat in a large non-stick skillet, then toss in the bread crumbs, parsley, and garlic. Cook until the bread crumbs are nicely browned, stirring occasionally, and the mixture is fragrant. Turn off the heat and let it cool a bit, then season with salt and pepper.

2 Spread 1 teaspoon or so of the remaining butter around the bottom of 9 × 13-inch baking dish, then arrange the shrimp in the dish; sprinkle with salt and pepper. Cover with about half the bread crumb mixture, then arrange the tomatoes on top. Sprinkle with the remaining bread crumbs and dot with the remaining butter. Bake until the shrimp are pink and hot, 8 to 12 minutes, depending on the size of the shrimp.

Sautéed Scallops

Scallops are best when their interiors are left underdone. To avoid overcooking, it's best to remove the scallops from the pan after an initial browning, then return them—just to reheat once the sauce is made.

Makes 4 servings

Time: 15 minutes, more or less

2 tablespoons olive oil

1 teaspoon minced garlic

1 to 1½ pounds scallops, preferably sea or bay

Salt and freshly ground black pepper to taste

Juice of 1 lemon

1 tablespoon minced fresh chives

1 Heat a large non-stick skillet over medium-high heat for 3 or 4 minutes; add the olive oil, garlic, and, 30 seconds later, the scallops, a few at a time. Turn them as they brown, allowing about 2 minutes per side (less for scallops under an inch across, somewhat more for those well over an inch). Season them with salt and pepper as they cook; remove them to a bowl as they finish.

2 Add the lemon juice to the liquid in the pan and cook over medium-high heat until the liquid is reduced to a glaze, 1 or 2 minutes. Return the scallops to the skillet, along with the chives, and stir to coat with the sauce and reheat, 1 to 2 minutes. Serve immediately.

Buttery Scallops In Step 1, preheat the skillet for just 2 minutes; replace all or half the oil with butter. Don't brown the scallops; keep the heat at medium, and cook them on both sides until they are opaque. In Step 2, add 1 teaspoon minced fresh tarragon leaves or ½ teaspoon dried tarragon, along with the lemon juice, salt, and pepper. Finish as above, stirring in 1 teaspoon of butter with the scallops (omit the chives) and garnish with minced chervil, tarragon (just a little), or parsley leaves.

Ginger Scallops In Step 1, use peanut or vegetable oil. Add 1 tablespoon peeled and minced or grated fresh ginger with the garlic. Add 3 chopped scallions to the skillet with the scallops. In Step 2, use a mixture of 1 tablespoon soy sauce, 1 tablespoon dry sherry or white wine, and 2 tablespoons water, chicken, fish, or vegetable stock in place of the lemon juice. Finish with chives or some minced scallions, and add salt and pepper if necessary.

Warm Salad of Scallops and Tender Greens

You can make this with shrimp as well; slice them in half the long way and cook just 1 minute per side.

Makes 4 servings

Time: About 15 minutes

2 tablespoons freshly squeezed lemon juice

3 tablespoons peanut or other oil

1 tablespoon minced shallot

1 tablespoon water

Salt and freshly ground black pepper to taste

1 pound sea scallops, cut in half horizontally

6 cups torn tender greens, such as Boston lettuce or mâche, or a mixture (trimmed, washed, and dried)

1   Whisk together the lemon juice, 1½ tablespoons of the oil, the shallot, and the 1 tablespoon of water in a small bowl. Season with salt and pepper.

2   Heat the remaining oil in a large non-stick skillet over high heat. Add the scallops and sear until golden, 2 to 3 minutes per side.

3   Toss the greens with half of the dressing in a large bowl. Divide the salad among four plates, arrange the scallops over the salad, and drizzle the remaining dressing over them. Serve immediately.

4 | Poultry

Broiled or Grilled Chicken with Pesto   50

   🕐 Pesto   51

   🕐 Garlic Butter   51

   🕐 Chile Oil   51

🕐 Sautéed Chicken Cutlets   52

Grilled or Broiled Chicken Cutlets   53

Herb-Roasted Chicken Cutlets   54

🕐 Crunchy Curried Chicken Breasts   55

Chicken in Lemon Sauce   56

Chicken Satay   57

Stir-Fried Chicken with Broccoli or Cauliflower   58

Chicken Wings with Black Bean Sauce   59

Chicken or Duck Salad with Walnuts   60

Curried Chicken Salad   61

🕐 20 minutes or less

Broiled or Grilled Chicken with Pesto

Broiled or grilled chicken has almost infinite variations. It is fabulous flavored with pesto, but you can also cook it with almost any compound butter, such as Garlic Butter (at right) or flavored oil, such as Chile Oil (at right). If you make pesto and flavored oils in advance, you can have them ready for a quick meal anytime.

Makes 4 servings

Time: 20 to 30 minutes, plus time to preheat the grill

½ to 1 cup Pesto (at right)

1 whole (3- to 4-pound) chicken, cut up (legs cut in two), trimmed of excess fat, then rinsed and patted dry with paper towels

Salt and freshly ground black pepper to taste

Lemon wedges

1   Start a charcoal or wood fire or preheat a gas grill or broiler. The fire should not be too hot, and the rack should be at least 6 inches from the heat source.

2   If you're broiling, spread a tablespoon or so of the pesto on a non-stick broiling or baking pan; place the chicken pieces on top and sprinkle them with salt and pepper. Spread a little more of the pesto on the chicken. If you're grilling, spread some of the pesto all over the chicken.

3   Broil or grill the chicken, turning and basting frequently with the pesto, until nicely browned all over and cooked through (the juices will run clear if you make a small cut in the meat near the bone), 20 to 30 minutes. Brush once more with the pesto and serve hot or at room temperature (refrigerate if you will not be serving it within the hour), with lemon wedges.

Shopping Tip: Start with a high-quality chicken, preferably free-range chicken or Kosher (unfortunately, the word "natural" doesn't mean much). Either of these will have more flavor than commercial chickens, though they'll also be somewhat more expensive.

Preparation Tip: Cook chicken quickly, use cut-up chicken, or cut it up yourself. Be sure to separate the leg and thigh; that joint (easy to find, and easy to cut through) is the slowest cooking part of the bird if you leave it intact.

Broiled or Grilled Chicken with Lemon and Herbs   Omit the pesto. Loosen the skin of each piece of chicken (use a paring knife if necessary to separate skin from meat) and insert a bit of fresh herb—a leaf of sage, tarragon, or basil, or a few pieces of rosemary, chervil, or thyme—between the skin and the meat. Rub the chicken all over with freshly squeezed lemon juice and sprinkle it liberally with salt and pepper to taste. Cook as in Step 3, brushing with more lemon juice from time to time. Garnish with minced fresh herbs and serve with lemon wedges.

Pesto

Makes about 1 cup • Time: 5 minutes

You can make pesto thick or thin by adding oil until you like the texture.

2 loosely packed cups fresh basil leaves, big stems discarded, rinsed, and dried	2 tablespoons pine nuts or walnuts, lightly toasted in a dry skillet
Salt to taste	1/2 cup extra-virgin olive oil, or more
1/2 to 2 cloves garlic, crushed	1/2 cup freshly grated Parmesan or other hard cheese (optional)

Combine the basil, salt, garlic, nuts, and about half the oil in a blender. Process, stopping to scrape down the sides of the container occasionally, and adding the rest of the oil gradually. Add additional oil if you prefer a thinner mixture. Store in the refrigerator for a week or two, or in the freezer for several months. Stir in the Parmesan by hand just before serving.

Garlic Butter

Makes 4 to 8 servings • Time: 10 minutes

Use this on broiled or grilled meats or fish, on baked potatoes, rice, barley, or other grains, or on noodles.

1 tablespoon butter	Salt and freshly ground black pepper to taste
1 teaspoon minced garlic	
4 tablespoons (1/2 stick) butter, at room temperature	Freshly squeezed lemon juice to taste

Melt 1 tablespoon butter in a small saucepan over low heat; add the garlic and cook just until the garlic softens, 2 or 3 minutes. Let cool. Cream with softened, room-temperature butter; add salt, pepper, and lemon juice.

Chile Oil

Makes about 1/2 cup • Time: 15 minutes

A medium-hot sauce that is super for basting anything you are grilling.

1 dried ancho or other not overly hot chile	1/4 cup corn, peanut, olive, or vegetable oil
2 teaspoons salt	

Toast the chile on the grill or under the broiler for 1 minute. Turn and grill chile for another minute, until it is soft and fragrant; keep an eye on it so that it does not burn. Remove the chile and cool, then cut off and discard the stem. Place the chile and its seeds in a spice grinder and pulverize into a fine powder. Combine the powder with salt and stir it into the oil. You can refrigerate this indefinitely.

Sautéed Chicken Cutlets

This is among the simplest of recipes: It has no sauce and virtually no seasonings. But, given good chicken and care not to overcook, it is delicious.

Makes about 4 servings

Time: 20 minutes

4 boneless, skinless chicken cutlets (2 breasts), 1 to 1½ pounds, rinsed and patted dry with paper towels

Salt and freshly ground black pepper to taste

1 cup all-purpose flour, plain bread crumbs, or cornmeal

2 tablespoons olive oil

1 tablespoon butter (or use all olive oil)

Lemon wedges

Minced fresh parsley leaves for garnish (optional)

1 Heat a large skillet, preferably non-stick, over medium-high heat for 2 or 3 minutes. While it is heating, sprinkle the chicken breasts with salt and pepper and place the flour, bread crumbs, or cornmeal on a plate or in a shallow bowl.

2 Add the oil and butter, if any, to the skillet and swirl it around. When it is hot—a pinch of flour will sizzle—dredge a piece of the chicken in the coating, pressing it down a bit to coat evenly. Shake it a little so that excess coating falls off. Add the chicken piece to the pan, then move on to the next one. (Don't dredge in advance and add all the pieces at once; the coating will become soggy, and the pan heat will drop too quickly.)

3 Cook the chicken, regulating the heat if necessary so that there is a good constant sizzle but no burning. After 2 minutes, rotate the chicken (do not flip) so that the outside edges are moved toward the center and vice versa. After 3 to 4 minutes, when the pieces are brown, turn them over.

4 Cook on the second side 3 to 4 minutes, until the chicken breasts are firm to the touch. If you are unsure whether they're done, cut into one with a thin-bladed knife; the center should be white (the barest trace of pink is okay, too—they will finish cooking on the way to the table). Serve with lemon wedges; garnish with parsley if you like.

Spice-Coated Chicken Cutlets Before coating the chicken, combine the flour or cornmeal with 1 tablespoon chili powder, curry powder, five-spice powder, or ground cumin. Proceed as above, using all oil (peanut or vegetable oil is best in this case) and garnishing with lime wedges rather than lemon.

Sesame-Coated Chicken Cutlets Use sesame seeds or ground nuts as the coating, instead of flour, cornmeal, or bread crumbs, pressing well to help them adhere. Proceed as above, using all oil (peanut or vegetable oil is best in this case), and cooking over slightly lower heat to avoid burning. (Increase the cooking time by 1 to 2 minutes.) Finish, if you like, with a drizzle of dark sesame oil, a sprinkling of lime, and a few minced cilantro leaves.

Grilled or Broiled Chicken Cutlets

Easy cooking; easy eating. You can increase the recipe as needed, for more people or for leftovers—which makes for great sandwiches, quesadilla filling, you name it. Soy sauce makes a great non-fat basting liquid.

Makes 4 servings

Time: 20 minutes, plus time to preheat the grill

4 boneless, skinless chicken cutlets (2 breasts), 1 to 1½ pounds, rinsed and patted dry with paper towels

2 tablespoons soy sauce

Freshly ground black pepper to taste

1 tablespoon freshly squeezed lime juice

1 teaspoon dark sesame oil (optional)

1. Start a charcoal or wood fire or preheat a gas grill or broiler. The fire should not be too hot, but the rack should be fairly close to the heat source, 4 inches or less. If necessary, you can pound the chicken slices lightly between two pieces of waxed paper so that they are of uniform thickness.

2. Brush the chicken pieces with the soy sauce and sprinkle it with pepper. If you like, let the chicken marinate for 1 hour or more.

3. Grill or broil the chicken very quickly; it should take no more than 3 or 4 minutes per side. Sprinkle with lime juice and sesame oil; serve.

Cooking Tip: Overcooking boneless breasts—the most popular cut—is a real problem. Generally speaking, 6 minutes—3 per side—is sufficient time to cook a thin piece of chicken breast; 10 minutes will do for a plump piece. When it's done, the inside will be moist and a tiny bit pink, not dry and stark white.

Grilled or Broiled Chicken Cutlets in Sweet Soy Marinade ("Chicken Teriyaki")
In Step 2, immerse the chicken in a combination of 1 teaspoon dark sesame oil, ¼ cup soy sauce, 1 tablespoon peeled and finely minced or grated fresh ginger, ¼ cup minced scallion, both green and white parts, 1 teaspoon minced garlic, 1 tablespoon dry sherry, white wine, or water, and 1 tablespoon honey or sugar. (If you have extra time, marinate in refrigerator for 1 hour.) Remove the chicken from the marinade and boil the marinade for 1 minute. Grill or broil the chicken as in Step 3, brushing frequently with the marinade (omit the lime juice). Garnish with more minced scallion and serve.

Grilled or Broiled Chicken Cutlets with Herb Marinade In Step 2, combine 1 tablespoon olive oil (using a blender or food processor) with 2 to 4 tablespoons mixed fresh herbs—parsley, basil, tarragon—and a clove of garlic. Immerse the chicken in this mixture while the grill is heating. An hour marinating time will add flavor. Remove the chicken from the marinade and boil the marinade for 1 minute. Grill or broil the chicken as in Step 3, brushing frequently with the marinade. Garnish with more minced herbs and serve.

Herb-Roasted Chicken Cutlets

This is a terrific basic recipe, one in which the herb-scented crust of the chicken combines with stock to make a simple, delicious sauce.

Makes 4 servings

Time: 30 minutes

1 tablespoon minced fresh tarragon or summer savory, dill, parsley, or chervil leaves

¼ cup minced fresh parsley leaves, plus a little more for garnish

1 cup all-purpose flour

Salt and freshly ground black pepper to taste

3 tablespoons butter, olive oil, or a combination

4 boneless, skinless chicken cutlets (2 breasts), 1 to 1½ pounds, rinsed and patted dry with paper towels

1 cup chicken or vegetable stock, store-bought broth, or water, plus a little more if needed

1 Preheat the oven to 450°F. Mix together the herbs, flour, salt, and pepper. Heat a flame-proof baking dish over medium-high heat for 2 or 3 minutes, then add the butter and/or olive oil. When it is hot, dredge the chicken in the flour mixture, add it to the pan, and brown for a minute or so on each side. Add the stock or water and place the pan in the oven.

2 Roast the chicken, turning once or twice, until it is cooked through, about 6 to 10 minutes (if you are unsure whether the cutlets are done, cut into one with a thin-bladed knife; the center should be white or slightly pink). Remove the pan from the oven; transfer the chicken to a plate. If the juices remaining in the pan are thin, return the pan to the stove and cook over high heat for a minute or two to thicken them; if they're too thick, add a little more stock or water and cook over medium heat for a minute or two. Garnish the chicken and serve with some of the sauce spooned over it, and pass the remaining sauce at the table.

Cooking Tip: Because they are as close to a blank canvas as exists in food, chicken breasts showcase other flavors very, very well. Fresh herbs—especially tarragon, chervil, parsley, or other assertive but slightly sweet herbs—are ideal; dried herbs work well, too, but should be used in small doses as they quickly become overwhelming.

Crunchy Curried Chicken Breasts

This quick-to-make batter-coating, combined with shallow-frying in oil, yields an ultra-crisp crust. I like it spiked with curry powder, but you can use any spice blend. Alternatively, you can stir a handful of fresh herbs into the batter.

Makes 4 servings

Time: 20 minutes

4 boneless, skinless chicken cutlets
(2 breasts), 1 to 1½ pounds, rinsed and
patted dry with paper towels

1 tablespoon white or wine vinegar

Salt to taste

½ teaspoon freshly ground black pepper

1 tablespoon curry powder or other spice
mixture

1 cup all-purpose flour

½ cup warm water, plus more as needed

Peanut or vegetable oil as needed

Freshly squeezed lime juice or rice
vinegar or other mild vinegar

1 Rub the chicken all over with the vinegar. Combine the salt, pepper, and curry powder and rub this mixture into the chicken. In another bowl, mix the flour gradually with warm water, adding more water as necessary to make a paste the thickness of yogurt.

2 Heat a large skillet, preferably non-stick, over medium-high heat for 2 or 3 minutes. Add enough oil to the pan to reach a depth of about ⅛ inch. When the oil is hot (a pinch of flour will sizzle), dip each cutlet into the batter and place it in the skillet. Raise the heat to high and cook, regulating the heat if necessary so that there is a good constant sizzle but no burning. After 2 minutes, rotate the pieces (do not flip), so that the outside edges are moved toward the center and vice versa.

3 After 4 minutes, turn the pieces over. Cook until golden and crisp on each side, about 8 minutes total. Sprinkle with a little lime juice or vinegar and serve immediately.

Shopping Tip: As most experienced cooks know, curry powder is not a spice but a blend of spices (in India the related seasoning mix is called garam masala). You can make it yourself, to taste, but few non-Indians ever get to that point. Try to find a brand you like, and buy it fresh, replacing it about once a year even if it isn't used up; like all spices, it loses potency over time.

Chicken in Lemon Sauce

A simple, more-or-less traditional Provençal preparation, one that must be served with rice or good bread, or at least a spoon for the sauce.

Makes 4 servings

Time: 30 minutes

4 tablespoons (½ stick) butter or olive oil

2 leeks, washed well and diced, including some of the green part

½ cup dry white wine

½ cup chicken or vegetable stock, store-bought broth, or water, preferably warmed

½ teaspoon minced fresh thyme or tarragon leaves, or a good pinch dried thyme or tarragon

4 boneless, skinless chicken cutlets (2 breasts), 1 to 1½ pounds, rinsed and patted dry with paper towels, and cut into 1- to 1½-inch chunks

2 tablespoons freshly squeezed lemon juice

Salt and freshly ground black pepper to taste

Minced fresh parsley leaves for garnish

1 Melt 2 tablespoons of the butter or oil in a large skillet over medium heat. Add the leeks and cook, stirring, until softened, about 5 minutes. Add the wine, stock or water, and herb; bring to a boil and let bubble for a minute or two.

2 Add the chicken, turn the heat to medium-low, cover, and simmer until the meat is barely cooked through, 5 or 6 minutes. Remove the chicken with a slotted spoon and keep warm.

3 Turn the heat to high and cook the sauce rapidly, stirring occasionally, until just about ¾ cup remains; this will take 5 to 10 minutes. Lower the heat to medium-low, add the lemon juice, then stir in the remaining butter or oil, a bit at a time. If you're using oil, add it gradually, stirring vigorously with the back of a spoon as you do so.

4 Season with salt and pepper and return the chicken chunks to the sauce to heat through. Garnish and serve immediately.

Chicken Satay

This Indonesian grilled speciality gets great flavor from the marinade and dipping sauce. When sliced thinly for satays, chicken thighs are much less likely to dry out than breasts. They brown better, too. On non-rush days, you can marinate the meat in the refrigerator, up to 24 hours, for more flavor. Satays can also be made with meat or fish.

Makes 10 skewers, enough for 5 to 10 appetizers or 3 or 4 main-course servings

Time: 30 minutes

1 pound boneless chicken thighs rinsed and patted dry with paper towels

1/4 cup soy sauce

1/4 cup fish sauce (nuoc mam or nam pla, available at Asian markets), or use more soy sauce

1/2 cup water

1 teaspoon ground cumin

1 teaspoon ground coriander

1 tablespoon natural peanut butter or tahini (sesame paste)

1 teaspoon peeled and minced fresh ginger

1 tablespoon minced garlic

1 tablespoon sugar

1 tablespoon freshly squeezed lime or lemon juice or vinegar

1 Start a charcoal or wood fire or preheat a gas grill or broiler; the fire should be quite hot and the rack as close to the heat source as possible. Slice the chicken about 1/8 inch thick (it's easier if you freeze it for 15 to 30 minutes first). Mix together the remaining ingredients and stir in the chicken slices. Let sit to marinate until the fire is ready.

2 When you're ready to cook, thread the chicken onto skewers without crowding. Grill or broil until browned all over, a total of 5 to 8 minutes. While the meat is cooking, bring the marinade to a boil and reduce it slightly. Serve the skewers hot, using the marinade as a dipping sauce.

Stir-Fried Chicken with Broccoli or Cauliflower

Here is a model recipe for making stir-fry with "hard" vegetables, those that must be parboiled before stir-frying. The extra step actually saves time—it's much faster to soften broccoli and similar vegetables such as mushrooms or snow peas, with a quick poaching than by stir-frying.

Makes 4 servings, with rice

Time: 20 to 30 minutes

2 cups broccoli or cauliflower florets and stems, cut into bite-sized pieces

2 tablespoons peanut or other oil

2 tablespoons minced garlic

1 tablespoon peeled and grated fresh ginger

1 cup sliced onion

1/2 cup trimmed and chopped scallions, plus minced scallion greens for garnish

12 ounces boneless, skinless chicken breast, rinsed and patted dry with paper towels, cut into 1/2- to 3/4-inch chunks

1 teaspoon sugar (optional)

2 tablespoons soy sauce

Salt and freshly ground black pepper to taste

1 tablespoon hoisin sauce (optional; available at Asian markets)

1/2 cup toasted cashews (optional)

1 tablespoon cornstarch (optional)

1/4 cup chicken or vegetable stock or store-bought broth, or water

1 Bring a medium pot of salted water to a boil; add the broccoli or cauliflower and cook for about 2 minutes, just long enough to remove the hardest crunch. Drain and plunge into cold water to stop the cooking; drain again.

2 Place a wok or large, deep skillet over high heat. Add half the oil, swirl it around, and immediately add half the garlic and ginger. Cook for 15 seconds, stirring, then add the onion and cook, stirring, for 2 minutes. Add the broccoli or cauliflower and 1/2 cup chopped scallions and cook over high heat until the broccoli or cauliflower browns and becomes tender but not at all mushy, about 5 minutes.

3 Turn the heat to medium and remove the vegetables. Add the remaining oil to the pan, then the remaining garlic and ginger. Stir, then add the chicken. Raise the heat to high, stir the chicken once, then let it sit for 1 minute before stirring again. Cook, stirring occasionally, until the chicken has lost its pinkness, 3 to 5 minutes.

4 Return the vegetables to the pan and toss once or twice. Add the sugar, if desired, and the soy sauce, and toss again. Season with salt and pepper, then stir in the hoisin and cashews, if desired. If using, combine the cornstarch with the stock or water and add to the pan. Otherwise, just add the liquid. Raise the heat to high and cook, stirring and scraping the bottom of the pan, until the liquid is reduced slightly and you've scraped up all the bits of chicken. If you've used cornstarch, the sauce will have thickened.

5 Garnish and serve immediately, scooping out some of the sauce with each portion of meat and chicken.

Preparation Tip: To add variety and flavor to stir-fries, try (alone or in combination): a teaspoon of dark sesame oil, 1/2 to 1 cup raw or roasted cashews or peanuts, or 1 cup chopped shallots.

Chicken Wings with Black Bean Sauce

Chicken wings, once a cut that was ignored, have become super-popular, but we mostly see them grilled or deep-fried (and usually in restaurants and bars). Yet they make for a wonderful stir-fry and this recipe illustrates the basic technique; vary it at will.

Makes 4 servings

Time: 30 minutes

2 tablespoons fermented black beans

2 tablespoons dry sherry or white wine

1 tablespoon peanut or other oil

2 to 3 pounds chicken wings, rinsed and patted dry with paper towels, cut into 3 pieces, wing tips saved for stock

2 tablespoons minced garlic

1 tablespoon peeled and minced or grated fresh ginger

1/2 cup scallions (white and light green parts), cut into 1- to 2-inch lengths, plus minced scallion greens for garnish

2 tablespoons soy sauce

Freshly ground black pepper to taste

Salt to taste (optional)

1 tablespoon cornstarch (optional)

1/4 cup chicken or vegetable stock, store-bought broth, or water, preferably warmed

1 Soak the black beans in the sherry or wine. Heat a wok or large, deep skillet over medium-high heat for 3 to 4 minutes. Add the oil, swirl it around, and immediately add the chicken wings. Raise the heat to high and cook stirring and tossing occasionally, until browned and cooked through, 10 to 12 minutes. Remove the chicken with a slotted spoon and reduce the heat to medium.

2 Add the garlic and ginger to the skillet and cook for 15 seconds, stirring. Add the scallions and cook 30 seconds, stirring, just until they begin to wilt. Return the chicken to the pan.

3 Add the soy sauce, toss, then taste and add some pepper and some salt if necessary. Add the black beans and their soaking liquid. If you're using cornstarch, blend it with the stock or water and add it to the pan. If you're not using cornstarch, simply add the stock or water. Raise the heat to high and cook, stirring and scraping the bottom of the pan, until the liquid is reduced slightly and you've scraped all the bits of chicken off the pan. (If you've used cornstarch, the sauce will have thickened.)

4 Garnish with the minced scallions and serve immediately.

Shopping Tip: Fermented black beans are sold in every Chinese market and, because they are packed with loads of salt, keep indefinitely (unrefrigerated). Use them sparingly, as they are very strongly flavored.

Preparation Tip: Chicken wings have two joints; simply cut between them to create three pieces from each wing. The outermost tip should be saved for stock, as it has virtually no meat on it.

Chicken or Duck Salad with Walnuts

You can make this rich dish with the meat of any bird, from chicken to partridge; the stronger the flavor, the better the dish.

Makes 4 servings

Time: Less than 30 minutes

1 pound raw boneless skinless chicken meat, preferably from the thigh, or use duck or other meat

1 tablespoon canola or other neutral oil

2 tablespoons butter or olive oil

1 clove garlic, minced

1/2 cup walnuts or pecans, coarsely crumbled (do not chop)

1/4 cup port, crème de cassis, or sweet sherry or wine

4 to 6 cups torn assorted salad greens (trimmed, washed, and dried)

About 1/2 cup Vinaigrette (page 3)

A small handful minced fresh herb leaves, such as parsley or chervil, for garnish

1 Dice the chicken or other meat into 1/4- to 1/2-inch cubes.

2 Place the tablespoon of oil in a medium skillet and turn the heat to medium-high. A minute later, cook the meat in the oil, stirring, for about 4 minutes. Remove and set aside.

3 Wipe out the skillet and add the butter, still over medium-high heat; when the foam subsides, add the garlic and cook for 1 minute. Add the walnuts and stir for 30 seconds. Add the wine and let it bubble out until the mixture is syrupy, stirring occasionally. Turn off the heat and return the meat to the pan to warm it up.

4 Dress the greens with the vinaigrette and toss; add more vinaigrette if necessary. Scatter the meat and nut mixture on top of the greens, garnish, and serve.

Shopping Tips: You can usually find boneless chicken thighs in the supermarket, but if you cannot, and you don't wish to bone them yourself (it's intuitive, and quite simple), substitute boneless breasts.

You need not use vintage port for this recipe, but you need a sweet wine of some body and integrity. A decent tawny port will do the trick, and will keep for as long as it takes you to use (or drink) the rest of the bottle. Oloroso sherry would also be good.

Curried Chicken Salad

Poaching chicken in chicken stock improves both stock and chicken; you'll get delicious chicken for this salad, and great stock for the next time you need it. A delightful change from traditional chicken salad.

Makes 4 servings

Time: About 30 minutes

4 cups chicken or vegetable stock, store-bought broth, or water, preferably warmed

1 pound boneless skinless chicken breast (leftover chicken is fine; don't recook it), rinsed and patted dry with paper towels

1 tablespoon mayonnaise

1 tablespoon plain yogurt (or use more mayonnaise)

Salt and freshly ground black pepper to taste

1 tablespoon curry powder or garam masala or to taste

1/2 cup peeled and diced apple or 1/2 cup lightly toasted blanched slivered almonds

1 Place the stock in a medium saucepan and bring it to a boil over medium-high heat. Turn the heat to medium-low and add the chicken breast. Cook for about 10 minutes, or until the chicken breast is cooked through. Remove the meat; strain and reserve the stock for another use.

2 Cool the chicken, cut it into small pieces, and toss it with the remaining ingredients. Taste, correct seasoning, and serve.

Shopping Tip: Curry powder is a spice blend that includes cumin, black pepper, and ground chile powder, among other spices, including turmeric, which gives it its yellow color; garam masala is a brown spice blend with a spicy-sweet edge from ground cinnamon, cardamom, and cloves. Look for them in Indian and Asian markets, although now they can often be found in supermarkets. Try different brands to find your preferred blend.

5 | Meat

Grilled Steak   64

◔ Pan-Seared Steak with Red Wine Sauce   66

Stir-Fried Beef with Onions   67

Stir-Fried Spicy Beef with Basil   68

Beef Salad with Mint   69

Veal Cutlets, 1950s-Style   70

Sautéed Italian Sausage with Peppers and Onions   71

Sautéed Pork Chops   72

◔ Stir-Fried Pork with Spinach   74

◔ Sautéed Medallions of Pork with Lemon and Parsley   76

Grilled or Broiled Lamb Chops   77

◔ Lamb Medallions with Shallots, Tarragon, and Red Wine   78

Roast Rack of Lamb with Persillade   79

Lamburgers with Smoked Mozzarella   80

Bean Burritos with Meat   81

    ◔ Tomato-Onion Salsa   81

◔ 20 minutes or less

Grilled Steak

Straightforward and simple. Start with the right steak (prime meat, if you can find it, is definitely worth it) and don't over-cook. This is one of those times where a gas grill simply will not do the trick; you need a blazing hot fire and no cover if you want your steak crisp and slightly charred on the outside and rare inside; use real hardwood charcoal if at all possible. In this unusual case, pan-grilling is closer to grilling than broiling, since most home broilers just don't get hot enough.

Makes 2 to 4 servings

Time: About 10 minutes, plus time to preheat the grill

2 sirloin strip, rib-eye, or other steaks, 8 ounces each and about 1 inch thick

Salt and freshly ground black pepper to taste

1 Remove the steaks from the refrigerator and their packaging if you have not already done so. Build a medium-hot charcoal fire; you should not be able to hold your hand 3 inches above it for more than 2 or 3 seconds. The rack should be 3 or 4 inches from the top of the coals.

2 Dry the steaks with paper towels. Grill them without turning for 3 minutes (a little more if they're over an inch thick, a little less if they're thinner or you like steaks extremely rare). Turn, then grill for 3 minutes on the other side. Steaks will be rare to medium-rare.

3 Check for doneness. If you would like the steaks better done, move them away from the most intense heat and grill another minute or two longer per side; check again. When done, sprinkle with salt and pepper and serve.

Shopping Tip: *Strip steaks* are usually sold boneless and make the ideal individual steaks. *Rib-eyes*, the boneless center of the rib, are also very tender and very flavorful, and make good individual steaks. *Skirt steaks*, if you can find them (actually the steer's diaphragm), are a great steak, though they becomes extremely tough if cooked beyond medium-rare.

Broiled Steak A broiler is little more than an upside-down grill. The major difference is that melting fat can build up in your broiling pan and catch fire, so it's best to broil on a rack. Turn the broiler to maximum, preheat it, and broil 3 to 4 inches from the heat source (any more, and you won't brown the steak; any less, and you'll burn it). Proceed as for grilling, with this exception: If your broiler heat is not intense enough to brown the steak well, don't turn it, but cook it the entire time on one side only. It will cook reasonably evenly, and should develop a nice crust on the top.

Pan-Grilled Steak A terrific option for 1-inch-thick steaks (not much thicker, though), as long as you have a decent exhaust fan. Preheat a cast-iron or other sturdy skillet just large enough to hold the steaks over medium-high heat for 4 to 5 minutes; the pan should be really hot—in fact, it should be smoking. Sprinkle its surface with coarse salt and put in the steaks. Clouds of smoke will instantly appear; do not turn down the heat. The timing remains the same as for grilled steaks.

Tuscan Steak Drizzle some flavorful extra-virgin olive oil over the steak when it is done; top with freshly squeezed lemon juice to taste.

18 Quick Dishes Great for Entertaining

Many quick dishes can be great for entertaining, too. All of the dishes here are not only fast, but will also impress your guests.

Frittata, page 8

Cheese Quesadillas, page 9

Lightning-Quick Fish Soup, page 15

Fettuccine with Spinach, Butter, and Cream, page 22

Red Snapper or Other Fillets in Packages with Spinach, page 39

Grilled Mesclun-Stuffed Tuna or Swordfish Steaks, page 40

Salmon Roasted in Butter, page 42

Warm Salad of Scallops and Tender Greens, page 47

Chicken or Duck Salad with Walnuts, page 60

Pan-Seared Steak with Red Wine Sauce, page 66

Lamb Medallions with Shallots, Tarragon, and Red Wine, page 78

Roast Rack of Lamb with Persillade, page 79

Rice with Fresh Herbs, page 85

Crisp-Cooked Asparagus, page 94

Chard with Pine Nuts and Currants, page 97

Raspberry Fool, page 107

Strawberries with Balsamic Vinegar, page 108

Chocolate Mousse, page 111

Pan-Seared Steak with Red Wine Sauce

Few elegant, impressive dishes are as fast as this—*steak au poivre*. If you use tenderloin, you'll really need the sauce because the meat is so lean. If you use sirloin or rib-eye, the peppercorns and butter alone will be delicious (although the sauce won't hurt). If you have time, for extra flavor, coat the steaks with the peppercorns an hour or so before cooking and let them sit at room temperature.

This recipe is easily varied; use any spice rub in place of the black peppercorns.

Makes 4 servings

Time: 15 minutes

---

4 tenderloin steaks (filet mignon or "tournedos"), 4 to 6 ounces each, or use sirloin strip or rib-eye

Freshly ground black pepper, or a mixture of black pepper and crushed (see Step 2) allspice berries

3 tablespoons butter (preferred) or olive oil

1 tablespoon minced shallots

¾ cup zinfandel or other good red wine

2 sprigs fresh tarragon or ¼ teaspoon dried tarragon, plus fresh sprigs for garnish (optional)

Salt to taste

1. Preheat a large skillet over medium heat for about 3 minutes; turn the oven to 200°F.

2. Sprinkle steaks liberally with pepper. For genuine steak au poivre, coarsely grind about 1 tablespoon of pepper or pepper mixture and press into the meat. (About 1 part ground allspice berries to 3 parts pepper lends an interesting dimension.)

3. Put 2 tablespoons of the butter into the skillet; when the foam subsides, turn the heat to medium-high and put in the steaks. Cook the steaks for about 3 minutes per side for rare meat, a bit longer if you like it medium to well done. Undercook them a bit as they will continue to cook in the oven.

4. Remove the steaks to an ovenproof platter and place the platter in the oven. Over medium heat, add the remaining butter to the pan, along with the shallots. Stir until the shallots soften, about 1 minute.

5. Add the wine and the tarragon, raise the heat to high, and let most of the liquid bubble away. Pour any juices that have accumulated around the steaks into the sauce and add salt to taste. Spoon the sauce over the steaks and serve, garnished with additional tarragon if you like.

Shopping Tip: Any wine you use in cooking should be good enough to drink. It need not be expensive or esoteric, but neither should it be the so-called "cooking wine" sold in supermarkets. Decent red wine makes a difference here; zinfandel, for example, has a spicy fruitiness that complements the tarragon and shallots nicely.

Cooking Tip: Use a skillet that will fit the steaks comfortably, without either crowding them (which will cause them to steam rather than brown) or leaving too much room, which will allow the butter to burn.

Stir-Fried Beef with Onions

Onions, beef, and ginger are an almost holy combination; the synthesis is simply delicious. Flank and sirloin steaks are the cuts of choice here, though you can use less expensive cuts, like round, if you make the slices very thin.

Makes 4 servings

Time: 30 minutes

¾ to 1 pound flank or sirloin steak, or other beef

Salt and freshly ground black pepper to taste

2 tablespoons peanut (preferred) or vegetable oil

2 large or 3 medium onions, thinly sliced

1 teaspoon minced garlic

1 tablespoon peeled and minced or grated fresh ginger, plus 1 teaspoon

½ cup beef or chicken stock, store-bought broth, or water

1 tablespoon hoisin sauce (available in Asian markets) or soy sauce

1 Slice the beef as thinly as you can; it's easier if you freeze it for 15 to 30 minutes first. Cut the slices into bite-sized pieces. Season with salt and pepper and set aside.

2 Heat a wok or large skillet over high heat until it smokes. Add 1 tablespoon of oil and the onions. Stir immediately, then stir every 30 seconds or so until the onions soften and begin to char slightly, 4 to 5 minutes. Season the onions with salt and pepper, then remove them; keep the heat high.

3 Add the remaining oil to the pan, then the garlic and 1 tablespoon of ginger; stir and immediately add the beef. Stir immediately, then stir every 20 seconds or so until it loses its color, just a minute or two longer; stir in the onions. Add the stock or water, the hoisin or soy, and the remaining ginger; let some of the liquid bubble away and serve immediately, over rice.

Stir-Fried Beef with Tomatoes and Black Beans In Step 1, soak the sliced meat in 2 tablespoons soy sauce while you get everything else ready. At the same time, soak 1 tablespoon fermented black beans in 2 tablespoons dry sherry (or use stock, white wine, or water). Step 2 remains the same. In Step 3, add 3 or 4 scallions, including some of the green parts, cut into 1-inch lengths, along with the garlic and ginger. Add the beef and soy sauce, cook for 1 minute, then add 3 medium tomatoes, cored and roughly chopped (peel and seed the tomatoes if you like), then add the black beans and their liquid and the onions. Omit the stock and hoisin sauce. Stir, taste for salt and pepper, and serve immediately, over rice.

Stir-Fried Spicy Beef with Basil

Once you get this Thai-style dish set up, it's so quick to make that if you're serving it with rice, you should have the rice finished before you begin stir-frying. You can use beef round or chuck here, but the best cuts are flank or sirloin, which are more tender and equally tasty. Tenderloin, another possibility, will not give you as much flavor but will be supremely tender.

Makes 4 to 6 servings

Time: 15 to 30 minutes

1½ pounds flank or sirloin steak, or other beef cut

½ cup loosely packed basil leaves

1 tablespoon peanut oil, plus 1 teaspoon (optional)

1½ tablespoons minced garlic

¼ teaspoon crushed red pepper flakes, or to taste

1 tablespoon soy sauce or fish sauce (nam pla or nuoc mam, available at Asian markets)

Juice of ½ lime

1 Slice the beef as thinly as you can, across the grain; it's easier if you freeze it for 15 to 30 minutes first. Cut the slices into bite-sized pieces.

2 Wash and dry the basil; if the leaves are large, chop them coarsely. If time permits, mix the beef, basil, and the teaspoon of peanut oil in a bowl, cover, and refrigerate for 10 minutes. (Although far from essential, this helps the flavor of the basil permeate the meat).

3 When you are ready to cook, have all ingredients ready (including a serving dish and rice, if any). If you have not yet done so (in Step 2), mix together the beef and basil. Preheat a wok or a large skillet over high heat until it smokes, 3 or 4 minutes.

4 Lower the heat to medium and add the tablespoon of peanut oil to the wok. Swirl it around and add the garlic. Stir once or twice. As soon as the garlic begins to color—about 15 seconds—return the heat to high and add the beef-basil mixture. Stir quickly and add the red pepper. Stir frequently (but not constantly), just until the meat loses its redness, a minute or two longer. Add soy sauce and lime juice, stir, turn off heat, and serve immediately.

Shopping Tip: *Nam pla*—Thai fish sauce, called *nuoc mam* in Vietnam—is little more than fish, salt, and water, and an ancient way of preserving fish and adding its flavor to foods long after the catch is made. It's strong-flavored (and even stronger-smelling) but a great and distinctive substitute for soy sauce.

Beef Salad with Mint

This is a meaty salad, a nice compromise between eating a huge cut of steak and none at all. The salad is a Southeast Asian classic, even a staple, but the frequency with which it's served is justifiable.

Makes 3 to 4 light servings

Time: 25 minutes, plus time to preheat the grill

1 (8- to 10-ounce) piece beef tenderloin (such as filet mignon) or sirloin

4 cups torn Boston or romaine lettuce, mesclun, or any salad greens mixture (trimmed, washed, and dried)

1/4 cup minced fresh mint, parsley, basil, or cilantro leaves

1 small red onion, sliced into thin rings

1 small cucumber, preferably unwaxed and unpeeled, thinly sliced

4 tablespoons freshly squeezed lime juice

1 tablespoon fish sauce (nuoc mam or nam pla, available at Asian markets) or soy sauce

1/8 teaspoon cayenne, or to taste

1/2 teaspoon sugar

1 If you are starting with raw meat, start a charcoal or wood fire or preheat a gas grill or broiler; the rack should be about 4 inches from the heat source. Grill or broil the beef until medium-rare, about 10 to 12 minutes; set it aside to cool.

2 Toss the lettuce with the mint, onion, and cucumber. Combine all remaining ingredients, and toss the greens with this mixture, reserving about 1 tablespoon of the dressing.

3 Slice the beef thinly, reserving its juice; lay the slices over the salad. Mix the juice and reserved dressing, drizzle over the beef, and serve.

Cooking Tip: You can grill the beef well ahead of time and slice it at the last minute. All beef (and most meat) slices more easily, and retains more of its juice, if you let it rest for a little while—5 to 10 minutes—before carving. Since this is a salad, and not really a hot dish, it's the perfect opportunity to try this out.

Veal Cutlets, 1950s-Style

Before we "discovered" boneless chicken breasts, thin slices of veal cut from the leg—called cutlets, scallops, or scallopine—were the only thin, tender, boneless meat widely available. But veal was expensive, and remains so. Still, veal does have a different texture and flavor than chicken breasts, and good veal cutlets are still wonderful sautéed in olive oil and drenched in lemon juice. You can make this recipe with thinly pounded chicken or turkey cutlets, or with any thin-sliced pork.

Makes 4 servings

Time: 30 minutes

1¼ to 1½ pounds thinly sliced veal, from the leg (scallopine)

¼ cup olive oil, or a little more

Flour for dredging

Plain bread crumbs for dredging

2 eggs

Salt and freshly ground black pepper to taste

½ cup dry white wine

Juice of 1 lemon

Minced fresh parsley leaves for garnish

1 lemon, cut into quarters

1   The cutlets should be less than ¼ inch thick; if they're not, pound them gently (I use a flat rolling pin, but you can use the back of a skillet or a wine bottle) between two sheets of waxed paper.

2   Heat the olive oil in a large skillet over medium heat while you set out the flour and bread crumbs on plates and beat the eggs lightly in a small bowl. Season the flour liberally with salt and pepper.

3   When the oil is good and hot (a pinch of flour will sizzle), dredge the cutlets, one at a time, in the flour, then dip in the egg, then dredge in the bread crumbs. Add them to the skillet as they're ready. Cook them over heat high enough to make the oil bubble; don't crowd. Cook in batches if necessary, adding additional oil as needed. Set the oven at 200°F.

4   Turn the cutlets as they brown, then cook the other side. The total cooking time should be 5 minutes or less. As each piece is done, remove it to an ovenproof platter; place the platter in the oven.

5   When all the veal is finished, pour off the fat. Return the skillet to the stove and add the wine, over medium-high heat. Cook, stirring, until the wine is just about evaporated. Add the lemon juice, stir, and pour this sauce (there won't be more than a few tablespoons) over the veal. Garnish and serve, passing lemon quarters at the table.

Veal Cutlets with Rosemary and Parmesan Here, you can skip the flour-and-egg treatment and dredge directly in a bread crumb–Parmesan mixture; the results will be very good. Combine ½ cup freshly grated Parmesan cheese, ½ cup plain bread crumbs, 1 tablespoon minced fresh rosemary leaves or 1 teaspoon dried rosemary, and some salt and pepper in a bowl. In Step 3, dredge in flour and egg if you like, or omit this step. In any case, finish by dredging the cutlets in the bread crumb–Parmesan mixture. Proceed as above, skipping Step 5 and serving the veal with lemon quarters as soon as it's cooked.

Sautéed Italian Sausage with Peppers and Onions

There are two ways to proceed here: Cook the vegetables in olive oil first, then combine them with the sausage after browning, or cook the sausages first, then use the sausage fat to cook the vegetables. The first method cuts saturated fat, the second boosts flavor—it's your choice. I detail the first method here; to do the second, simply cook the sausage, as directed, remove the sausages to a plate, leave the fat in the pan, and cook the vegetables in it.

Sausages cooked this way are fantastic between two thick slices of good bread, or inserted into a lengthwise-cut loaf of French or Italian bread. Strong mustard is the natural accompaniment.

Makes 4 servings

Time: About 30 minutes

2 cups sliced onions

3 tablespoons olive oil

2 bell peppers, any color but green, stemmed, peeled if desired, seeded, and cut into strips

Salt and freshly ground black pepper to taste

1 pound fresh link Italian sausage, sweet or hot

1   Place the onions in a large skillet, turn the heat to medium, cover the pan, and cook, undisturbed, for about 5 minutes, until the onions are dry and almost sticking to the pan. Remove the cover, add the oil, and stir. Cook for a minute or two longer, then add the peppers, salt, and pepper. Cook, stirring frequently, until the vegetables are tender and soft, about 10 more minutes. Remove the vegetables and keep warm.

2   Cook the sausage in the same pan over medium heat. Prick the sausage in a few places with a fork to allow excess fat to escape and turn the sausage frequently. Cook until nicely browned all over. Total cooking time will depend on the thickness of the sausages; the best way to determine doneness is to cut into one—when the barest trace of pink remains, they are done. Drain the sausages on a paper towel and serve with the peppers and onions.

Sautéed Pork Chops

A straightforward, simple method of cooking pork chops that always gives good results, no matter what seasonings you add. Use center-cut loin chops if at all possible. This will become a favorite; try the variations, too.

Makes 4 servings

Time: 30 minutes

4 center-cut loin pork chops, about 1 inch thick, trimmed of excess fat

Salt and freshly ground black pepper to taste

2 tablespoons olive oil, plus more if not using butter

$1/2$ cup dry white wine

1 teaspoon minced garlic or 2 tablespoons minced shallot, onion, or scallion

$1/2$ cup chicken, beef, or vegetable stock, store-bought broth, or water, plus more if needed

1 tablespoon butter (you can use more olive oil instead, especially if it's flavorful)

1 tablespoon freshly squeezed lemon juice or wine vinegar

Minced fresh parsley leaves for garnish

1 Sprinkle the chops with salt and pepper. Place a large skillet over medium-high heat for 2 or 3 minutes. Add the 2 tablespoons olive oil; as soon as the first wisps of smoke rise from the oil, add the chops and turn the heat to high. Brown the chops on both sides, moving them around so they develop good color all over. The entire browning process should take no longer than 4 minutes, and preferably less.

2 Reduce the heat to medium. Add the wine and the garlic and cook, turning the chops once or twice, until the wine is all but evaporated, about 3 minutes. Add $1/2$ cup of stock or water, turn the heat to low, and cover. Cook for 10 to 15 minutes, turning the chops once or twice, until the chops are tender but not dry. When done, they will be firm to the touch, their juices will run just slightly pink and, when you cut into them (which you should do if you're at all unsure of their doneness), the color will be rosy at first glance but quickly turn pale.

3 Remove the chops to a platter. If the pan juices are very thin, cook, stirring and scraping the bottom of the pan, until the liquid is reduced slightly. If they are scarce (unlikely), add another $1/2$ cup of stock or water; cook, stirring and scraping the bottom of the pan, until the liquid is reduced slightly. Then stir in the butter or oil over medium heat; add the lemon juice, pour over the chops, garnish, and serve.

Shopping Tip: A good pork chop contains some fat, and if you cannot find *center cut pork chops* that show some marbling, look for *shoulder* (also called *blade*) chops; *loin-end chops* are almost always too lean. Try to find chops that are at least an inch thick—you'll be much happier with one thick chop than two thin ones, which invariably overcook.

Pork Chops with Sherry-Garlic Sauce Steps 1 and 2 remain the same. In Step 3, after removing the chops, add 1/2 cup not-too-dry sherry (oloroso or amontillado) and cook, stirring and scraping the bottom of the pan, until the liquid is reduced slightly. Add 1 tablespoon olive oil and 1 tablespoon minced garlic and continue to cook until the liquid becomes syrupy. Omit butter. Stir in 1/4 cup minced fresh parsley leaves and the juice of 1/2 lemon. Taste for seasoning, pour over the chops, garnish and serve.

Pork Chops with Apples Steps 1 and 2 remain the same. In Step 3, after removing the chops, cook 2 cups peeled, cored, and sliced apples in the remaining liquid, stirring and scraping the bottom of the pan as the apples cook and adding about 1/2 cup more liquid (white wine or stock) if necessary. When the apple slices are soft, about 5 minutes, stir in 1 tablespoon lemon juice (omit butter), pour over the chops, garnish, and serve.

Pork Chops with Mustard Steps 1 and 2 remain the same. In Step 3, stir in 1 tablespoon or more of Dijon mustard with the lemon juice (some capers are good here, too, as is a dash or two of Worcestershire sauce). Finish as above.

Pork Chops with Onions and Peppers Steps 1 and 2 remain the same; undercook the chops slightly and preheat the oven to warm. In Step 3, after removing the chops, put them in the warm oven. Stir in 2 cups thinly sliced onions and 2 cups stemmed, seeded, and sliced peppers, any color but green. Stir, re-cover the pan, and cook for 5 minutes over medium heat. Remove the cover and cook, stirring, until the vegetables are softened and beginning to brown, about 5 more minutes. Moisten with 1/2 cup stock, then cook until most of the stock is absorbed. Omit butter. Stir in 1 tablespoon of lemon juice or vinegar, taste and adjust seasoning, and serve over the chops. A teaspoon of minced fresh marjoram, oregano, or thyme leaves (or 1/2 teaspoon of dried herb), or a tablespoon or two of minced fresh basil or parsley is good stirred into the vegetables just as they finish cooking.

Stir-Fried Pork with Spinach

A couple of pointers about this basic stir-fry: If you like a strong garlic flavor, reserve 1/2 tablespoon of the garlic and stir it in at the end of the cooking, along with the soy sauce and lime juice. And if the mixture is drier than you like after you've added the soy sauce and lime juice, add 1/4 to 1/2 cup of water or any stock or broth you have on hand; heat through and serve.

You can substitute any tender green when they are in season—arugula, cress, chard, or dandelion are all good—for the spinach. And add a small handful of chopped basil at the last minute if you like.

Makes 4 servings

Time: About 15 minutes

1 pound boneless pork, preferably from the shoulder, trimmed of external fat

About 1 pound spinach, trimmed and well washed

2 tablespoons peanut or other vegetable oil

1 1/2 tablespoons minced garlic

1 tablespoon soy sauce

Juice of 1/2 lime

1/2 cup minced scallion or 1/4 cup minced chives for garnish

1   Slice the pork as thinly as you can; it's easier if you freeze it for 15 to 30 minutes first. Cut the slices into bite-sized pieces, about the size of a quarter. Chop or tear the spinach coarsely.

2   When you're ready to cook, have all ingredients ready, including a serving dish and rice, if any. Preheat a wok or a large, heavy skillet over high heat until it begins to smoke. Immediately add 1 tablespoon of the peanut oil and the pork. Cook, stirring occasionally (not constantly), until the pork browns and loses all traces of pinkness, about 3 minutes. Use a slotted spoon to remove the pork to a bowl, and lower the heat to medium.

3   Add the remaining peanut oil to the wok. Swirl it around and add the garlic. Stir once or twice. As soon as garlic begins to color—about 15 seconds—return the heat to high and add the spinach. Stir frequently, just until the spinach wilts, a minute or two longer.

4   Add the pork and stir for 1 minute. Add the soy sauce and lime juice, stir, turn off the heat, garnish, and serve immediately.

Shopping Tip: Pork has become so lean that certain cuts—the tenderloin for example—have become practically tasteless. These days, the best cut for stir-fries and many other uses is the shoulder, which still contains enough fat to be flavorful.

Stir-Fried Pork with Sweet Onions In Step 1, use 3 cups peeled and sliced onions in place of spinach. In Step 3, cook the onions with the garlic, stirring over medium-high heat until they soften and begin to brown, 7 to 10 minutes. Sprinkle them with 1 teaspoon of sugar, then proceed to Step 4.

Stir-Fried Pork with Snow Peas and Ginger In Step 1, trim 2 cups of snow peas (or snap peas) in place of spinach. Step 2 remains the same. In Step 3, cook 2 tablespoons peeled and minced fresh ginger with the garlic, then add the snow peas, stirring over medium-high heat until they soften and begin to brown, about 5 minutes. In Step 4, add 1 teaspoon peeled and minced fresh ginger along with the soy sauce and lime juice.

3 Quick Additions to Pork Stir-Fries

1 Add 1/4 teaspoon or more crushed red pepper flakes along with the garlic.

2 Add 1 tablespoon of sugar to the pork as it cooks for added color, crispness, and sweetness.

3 Add 2 tablespoons whole or chopped peanuts or cashews along with the vegetables.

Sautéed Medallions of Pork with Lemon and Parsley

Medallions of pork are so thin that they cook through in the time it takes to brown them. Here's a basic recipe on which to build. Add a tablespoon or two of drained capers with the lemon juice if you like. You can follow any recipe for cutlets of veal (page 70) or chicken (pages 52–56) for pork medallions.

Makes 4 servings

Time: 15 minutes

1 (1- to 1¼-pound) pork tenderloin

¼ cup olive oil

Flour for dredging, liberally seasoned with salt and pepper

½ cup dry white wine

Juice of 1 lemon

Minced fresh parsley leaves for garnish

1 lemon, quartered

1 Cut the tenderloin into ½-inch-thick slices (it will be easier if you freeze the meat for about 30 minutes before cutting). Pound them gently (use a flat rolling pin, the back of a skillet, or a similar object) between two sheets of waxed paper to make them a bit thinner.

2 In a large skillet over medium heat, heat the olive oil; set the seasoned flour in a shallow bowl near the stove.

3 When the oil is good and hot (a pinch of flour will sizzle), dredge the medallions, one at a time, in the flour, then place them in the skillet. Cook them over heat high enough to make the oil bubble; don't crowd. Set the oven to 200°F.

4 Turn the pieces as soon as they're browned, then cook the other side; total cooking time should be 5 minutes or less, so adjust heat accordingly. As the meat is done, remove it to an ovenproof platter and place the platter in the oven.

5 When all the pork is finished, pour off the fat from the pan. Return the skillet to the stove and add the wine, over medium-high heat. Cook, stirring, until the wine is just about evaporated. Add the lemon juice, stir, and pour this sauce (there won't be more than a few tablespoons) over the meat. Garnish and serve, passing lemon quarters at the table.

Grilled or Broiled Lamb Chops

Like a simple strip sirloin steak, the lamb chop is a terrific convenience food—filling, fast, and, even without additions, flavorful. If you can get butcher-like service at your meat counter, or can visit a butcher, ask for double-rib chops, which are easier to cook to medium-rare, exactly how they should be. You can also pan-grill these in a skillet; see the Pan-Grilled Steak variation, page 65.

Makes 4 servings

Time: 15 minutes, plus time to preheat the grill

4 double-rib or large shoulder chops or 8 rib or loin chops

Salt and freshly ground black pepper to taste

1 clove garlic (optional)

Lemon wedges

1 Start a charcoal or wood fire or preheat a gas grill or broiler; the fire should be moderately hot for double chops, very hot for single chops. Sprinkle the meat with salt and pepper. If you like, cut the clove of garlic in half and rub it over the meat.

2 Grill or broil the chops, 3 or 4 inches from the heat source, until they are nicely browned on both sides. If they are single chops, allow no more than 2 or 3 minutes per side. With double chops, there is a greater margin for error, but cooking time will most likely still be less than 10 minutes. Serve with lemon wedges.

Shopping Tip: If you take a rack of lamb and cut it up, you get *lamb rib chops*, which are the most tender and least fatty. *Loin chops* are similar. Both rib and loin chops should be cooked rare to medium-rare. The far less expensive *shoulder chops*, however, are equally flavorful; you just have to discard a bit more gristle and fat and do a bit more chewing. In addition, they're better cooked a little longer, until just about medium.

Broiled or Grilled Lamb Chops, Italian-Style Use shoulder chops for this recipe, one per person (they're much bigger). Combine 1 tablespoon olive oil, 1 clove garlic, peeled, 2 or more anchovy fillets, 1/2 cup chopped fresh parsley leaves (plus more for garnish), 1 tablespoon freshly squeezed lemon juice, and some freshly ground black pepper to taste, and rub the chops with half of this mixture. If you have time, marinate for an hour or so (start the grill or broiler at the appropriate time, of course). Grill or broil as above, basting frequently with the remaining herb mixture, until nicely browned on both sides, a total of 6 to 8 minutes. Garnish and serve with lemon wedges.

Lamb Medallions with Shallots, Tarragon, and Red Wine

This dish has only a few ingredients, but they add up to a dish with a little something special. You may find lamb medallions precut, but better yet, ask the butcher to bone a rack of lamb for you, and don't let him discard the bones. Rather, use them for a simple lamb stock or just crisp them up in a very hot oven, sprinkle liberally with salt, and have them for a snack.

Makes 2 servings

Time: 20 minutes

1 boneless rack of lamb (lamb loin), about ½ pound

2 tablespoons butter (preferred) or olive oil

Salt and freshly ground black pepper to taste

1 tablespoon minced shallots

1 teaspoon minced fresh tarragon leaves or ¼ teaspoon dried tarragon

½ cup red wine

1 Cut the lamb into ¾-inch-thick rounds; there will be 6 or 8. Heat a large non-stick skillet over medium-high heat for 3 or 4 minutes. Heat the oven to 200°F.

2 Reserve 1 teaspoon of butter and add the rest to the pan; it should sizzle. Swirl the pan so the butter melts quickly and coats the pan evenly. Add the lamb medallions; sprinkle with salt and pepper and cook until brown on both sides, a total of 4 to 5 minutes. Turn the heat to low, remove the lamb to an ovenproof plate, and place in the oven.

3 Add the shallots to the pan. Cook, stirring, until the shallots are softened, about 2 minutes. Add the tarragon and wine, raise the heat to medium-high, and cook, stirring, until reduced by about half, about 5 minutes. Stir in the remaining butter. If any juices have seeped out of the lamb, add them to the pan, then spoon or pour the sauce over the lamb and serve.

Shopping Tip: This is a dish in which good red wine will stand out. As always, cook with something you would like to drink, but here—especially since the amount is so small—try to use something with real character—a good Bordeaux or other Cabernet will make a huge difference in the sauce.

Roast Rack of Lamb with Persillade

This is a great recipe for entertaining when you want to impress without spending much time in the kitchen. Rack of lamb is a luxury cut, delicious and virtually foolproof—as long as you don't overcook it. *Persillade* refers to the parsley-garlic flavoring, popularly used in southern France.

Makes 4 servings

Time: 30 minutes

2 racks of lamb, about 2 pounds each

2 tablespoons olive oil

Salt and freshly ground black pepper to taste

1 cup plain bread crumbs, preferably fresh

½ cup minced fresh parsley leaves

1 teaspoon minced garlic

1 Preheat the oven to 500°F. Trim the lamb of excess fat, but leave a layer of fat over the meat. Cut about halfway down the bones between the chops; this allows the meat between them to become crisp.

2 Combine all remaining ingredients and rub over the meat side of the racks. Put them in a roasting pan and place in the oven; roast for 20 minutes, and insert a meat thermometer straight in from one end into the meatiest part. If it reads 125°F or more, remove the lamb immediately. If it reads less, put the lamb back for 5 minutes, no more. Remove and let sit for 5 minutes. Serve, separating the ribs by cutting down straight between them.

Shopping Tips: Keep in mind that in a rack of lamb there are seven ribs per rack, and only a couple of bites per rib. You'll need two racks for four people, although, the fourteen ribs could serve five people in a pinch, and even six if there's plenty of other food and the crowd isn't ravenous.

Make sure the chine bone (backbone) is removed from the rack of lamb so you can easily cut through the ribs to separate them at the table, but don't bother to ask to have the ribs "frenched" (the meat removed from the top of the bones); the crisp meat along the bones is one of the pleasures of a rack of lamb.

Lamburgers with Smoked Mozzarella

Broil these, grill them, or pan-grill them. Any way you cook them, the outside will become crisp, the mozzarella will melt, and the inside will stay pink. A good way to wean kids from McDonald's.

Makes 4 servings

Time: 30 minutes, plus time to preheat the grill

Coarse salt (optional)

¼ pound smoked mozzarella

1 pound ground lamb, or a little more

Salt and freshly ground black pepper
to taste

1   Start a charcoal or wood fire or preheat a gas grill or broiler; the fire should be moderately hot. Or heat a large skillet over medium-high heat for 3 or 4 minutes before you start cooking, then sprinkle it with coarse salt.

2   Cut the cheese into 4 pieces and form the meat into patties around each one; season with salt and pepper.

3   Grill, broil, or pan-grill, 2 to 4 inches from the heat source, for about 3 or 4 minutes per side, or until the outside feels very firm. If you like your meat on the well-done side, move the burgers to a lower heat and cook an additional minute or two longer per side.

Cooking Tip: Ground lamb can be cooked longer than ground beef without suffering from dryness and toughness, but it should still be left somewhat pink inside.

Bean Burritos with Meat

Burritos are like a salad or a stew in a wrap—you can throw anything into the mix you like. For example, try substituting cooked and seasoned rice for the cheese.

Makes 6 servings

Time: 30 minutes with precooked beans

¾ to 1 pound ground meat or poultry, such as beef, turkey, or chicken, or a combination

½ cup chopped onion

1 tablespoon minced garlic

1 tablespoon chili powder, or to taste

About 2 cups Twice-Cooked ("Refried") Beans with Cumin (page 88) or other precooked or canned beans

Salt and freshly ground black pepper to taste

6 large flour tortillas

1½ to 2 cups grated Cheddar or jack cheese

2 cups washed, trimmed, dried, and chopped lettuce or other greens

Tomato-Onion Salsa (at right) or any spicy sauce or salsa

Minced cilantro leaves

1 Place the meat in a large skillet, preferably non-stick, and turn the heat to medium. Cook, stirring frequently, until the meat begins to lose its color. Stir in the onion and continue to cook, stirring, until the meat has lost all traces of pinkness and the lumps are broken up. Stir in the garlic and chili powder and cook for 1 minute longer.

2 Add the beans and cook, stirring, until they are warmed. Taste and add salt, pepper, and more chili powder if needed.

3 To warm the tortillas, wrap them in foil and place in a 300°F oven for about 10 minutes, or stack them between two damp paper towels and microwave for 30 to 60 seconds.

4 Spread a portion of cheese onto each tortilla and top with a portion of the bean-meat mixture, lettuce, salsa, and cilantro. Roll up and serve.

Tomato-Onion Salsa

Makes about 1 cup • Time: 10 minutes

This pureed salsa is great for burritos, and good as a sauce for chilled food, such as left-over grilled chicken.

1 medium onion, peeled

2 medium tomatoes, cored, peeled, and seeded

1 teaspoon paprika or ¼ to ½ teaspoon cayenne

1 clove garlic, peeled

1 tablespoon any good vinegar, plus more to taste

1 teaspoon salt, or to taste

1 teaspoon sugar

1 tablespoon freshly squeezed lemon juice, or to taste

1 Quarter the onion and tomatoes and whiz them in a food processor or blender with all the other ingredients except the lemon juice.

2 Taste and add more salt and paprika or cayenne if needed along with the lemon juice or vinegar to taste. Serve or refrigerate for up to a day or two before serving.

6 | Rice and Beans

Rice Pilaf   84

Rice with Fresh Herbs   85

🕐 Fried Rice with Greens   86

    🕐 Toasted Sesame Seeds   86

Chickpeas with Lemon   87

🕐 Twice-Cooked ("Refried") Beans with Cumin   88

Bean and Tomato Casserole   89

Black Beans with Crisp Pork and Orange   90

Black Beans and Rice, Spanish Style   91

🕐 20 minutes or less

Rice Pilaf

There are many definitions of pilaf, but two common features to all are: The rice must be briefly cooked in oil or butter before adding liquid, and the liquid must be flavorful. The oil or butter may be flavored with vegetables, herbs, or spices; the liquid may be anything from lobster stock to yogurt; and other foods may be added to the pot.

Makes 4 servings

Time: About 30 minutes

2 tablespoons butter or oil

1 cup chopped onion

1½ cups long-grain rice

Salt and freshly ground black pepper

2½ cups chicken, beef, vegetable stock, or store-bought broth, preferably warmed

Minced fresh parsley leaves for garnish

1 Place the butter or oil in a large, deep skillet, which can later be covered, and turn the heat to medium-high. When the butter melts or the oil is hot, add the onion. Cook, stirring, until the onion softens but does not begin to brown, 5 to 8 minutes.

2 Add the rice all at once, turn the heat to medium, and stir until the rice is glossy and completely coated with oil or butter, 2 or 3 minutes. Season well with salt and pepper, then turn the heat down to low and add the liquid, all at once. Cover the pan.

3 Cook for 15 minutes, then check the rice. When the rice is tender and the liquid is absorbed, it's done. If not, cook for 2 or 3 minutes and check again. Check the seasoning, garnish, and serve immediately.

Shopping Tip: The best rice for pilaf—and, generally speaking, the *ne plus ultra* of long-grain rice—is the wonderful Indian basmati, whose grains are even longer than that of other varieties, and whose nutty, beguiling aroma adds another dimension to cooking.

Pilaf with Raisins and Pine Nuts In Step 2, stir in ½ cup raisins or dried currants and ¼ cup pine nuts along with the rice. Finish as above.

Rice with Fresh Herbs

This is especially wonderful with butter and basmati or other aromatic rice.

Makes 4 servings

Time: About 30 minutes

2 tablespoons butter or oil

1/2 cup minced fresh chervil, basil, shiso, mint, parsley, cilantro, or other leafy herb, or a mixture

1 1/2 cups basmati or other long-grain rice

2 1/4 cups water

Salt and freshly ground black pepper to taste

1 Melt the butter over medium heat in a medium saucepan. Cook half the herb in the butter for 30 seconds. Add the rice and cook, stirring, until the rice is coated with butter.

2 Add the water and some salt and pepper. Turn the heat up a bit and bring the mixture to a boil. Cover and turn the heat to medium-low.

3 After 15 minutes, turn off the heat but leave the cover on the rice. Wait 10 minutes, then stir in the remaining herb. Check the seasoning and serve immediately.

Shopping Tip: Almost any herb will be delicious in this recipe, so it's a good place to experiment. If you can find chervil, a fragile herb that is not often sold in supermarkets, you'll be surprised at how delicious it is. Shiso, an herb popular in Mexico (where it's called *perilla*) and Japan (where it's served with sushi), is another good choice. But parsley, mint, or cilantro is also great here.

Fried Rice with Greens

This is a great way to use leftover rice (even rice that came with take-out food). It's a fine side dish, one that can easily steal the show; add a few bits of meat or fish and it becomes a solid main course. This is best with strong-flavored greens such as dandelion, mustard, or turnip. Be sure to wash and dry them very thoroughly.

Makes 4 servings

Time: 20 minutes or less with precooked rice

2 cups bitter greens, well washed and dried, all stems removed

3 tablespoons peanut (preferred) or canola or other oil

1 teaspoon minced garlic

1 teaspoon peeled and minced fresh ginger

2 tablespoons chopped scallion, plus minced scallion for garnish

1/4 teaspoon crushed red pepper flakes (optional)

3 to 4 cups leftover or cooked rice (any method is fine), cooled

2 tablespoons soy sauce

1 tablespoon oyster or hoisin sauce, or more soy sauce

Salt and freshly ground black pepper to taste

Toasted Sesame Seeds (at right) for garnish

1 Chop the greens roughly into fairly small pieces, with no dimensions larger than 2 inches. Place the oil in a wok or large skillet (preferably non-stick) and turn the heat to high. A minute later, add the garlic, ginger, chopped scallion, and red pepper and cook, stirring almost constantly, for 1 minute.

2 Turn the heat down a little bit and add the rice, a little at a time, crumbling it with your fingers to eliminate lumps if necessary. Stir frequently for about 1 minute, then add the greens. Cook, stirring frequently, until the greens become tender, about 3 minutes.

3 Add the soy sauce and oyster sauce and stir. Add salt and pepper if necessary. Garnish with sesame seeds and serve.

Toasted Sesame Seeds

Makes 1/2 cup • Time: 10 minutes

Sesame seeds should almost always be toasted before use; it brings out much more of their flavor. This same technique is useful for walnuts, almonds, pine nuts, and so on. Sesame seeds are best toasted just before using, but they will retain their fragrance for a few days if you wrap them tightly and refrigerate.

1/2 cup sesame seeds

1 Place the seeds in a dry skillet just large enough to contain them in one layer and turn the heat to medium.

2 Cook, shaking the pan frequently, until the seeds darken in color and begin to pop, 5 to 10 minutes. Cool slightly before using.

Chickpeas with Lemon

This chickpea salad is great to have around and a cinch with canned beans. Eat it warm, at room temperature, or cold—but add the lemon juice at the last minute for maximum flavor.

Makes 6 to 8 servings

Time: 30 minutes

4 cups cooked or canned chickpeas, drained

1 bay leaf

1 clove garlic, peeled

2 tablespoons minced shallot, onion, or scallion

3 tablespoons extra-virgin olive oil

Salt and freshly ground black pepper to taste

Freshly squeezed lemon juice to taste

Minced fresh parsley or cilantro leaves for garnish

1 Heat the chickpeas with the bay leaf and garlic and cook, stirring occasionally, for about 10 minutes.

2 Remove the bay leaf and garlic and drain. While the chickpeas are still warm, toss them with the shallot and olive oil and season with salt and pepper. (You may prepare this in advance up to this point; cover and refrigerate for up to a day, then bring to room temperature before proceeding.) Serve warm or at room temperature; just before serving add plenty of lemon juice and garnish.

Cooking Tip: For flavor or bulk, you can add cooked, crumbled ground meat, or a handful or two of good croutons.

Twice-Cooked ("Refried") Beans with Cumin

The traditional medium for frying beans is lard, and with good reason; it's delicious. But you can also make wonderful refried beans with oil.

Makes 4 servings

Time: 20 minutes with precooked beans

1/4 cup canola or other neutral oil

1 cup chopped onion

1 tablespoon ground cumin, plus more if desired

3 to 4 cups drained cooked or canned kidney or other red beans

Salt and freshly ground black pepper to taste

1/4 teaspoon cayenne, plus more if desired

1 Place the oil in a large skillet, preferably non-stick, and turn the heat to medium. When the oil is hot, add the onion and cook, stirring, until it is golden brown, about 10 minutes.

2 Add the cumin and cook, stirring, 1 minute more. Add the beans and mash with a large fork or potato masher. Continue to cook and mash, stirring, until the beans are more or less broken up (some remaining chunks are fine).

3 Season with salt and pepper, add the cayenne and more cumin if you like, and serve.

 Traditional Refried Beans   Substitute 1/2 cup lard for the oil and reserve the onion and cumin. Add the beans to the hot lard. When they are nicely mashed, stir in the onion and cumin and cook for 5 minutes more, stirring frequently. Season as above and serve.

Bean and Tomato Casserole

This is suitable as a main course. To make it even more so, add other vegetables, such as potatoes or cut-up greens; adjust the cooking time accordingly.

Makes 4 to 6 servings

Time: 30 minutes with precooked beans

6 cups drained cooked or canned beans, any type or a mixture

1 tablespoon chili powder, plus more to taste if desired

Salt and freshly ground black pepper to taste

2 tablespoons minced fresh savory, marjoram, or oregano leaves or about 20 fresh basil leaves, torn

4 medium-large tomatoes, sliced

2 large onions, sliced

1 cup grated jack or cheddar cheese

1 Preheat the oven to 400°F. Place the beans in a bowl, then stir the chili powder into the beans; taste and add more spice if you like.

2 In a baking dish or casserole, place a layer of beans; season with salt and pepper, and sprinkle with a little of the herb. Add a layer of tomatoes, one of onions, and a sprinkling of cheese. Repeat until all the ingredients are used up, finishing with a fairly thick layer of cheese.

3 Bake until the casserole is hot and the cheese melted and bubbly, about 20 minutes. Serve hot.

Black Beans with Crisp Pork and Orange

This is a simpler, liberal adaptation of the Brazilian *feijoada*, in which black beans are simmered with loads of meat: beef tongue and brisket, pork sausage, and pig's feet, plus—usually—a little salt pork thrown in for good measure. That dish, noble as it is, just doesn't appeal to that many people. This one, however, is more moderate, simpler, and equally tasty.

Makes 8 servings

Time: About 30 minutes with precooked beans

8 cups drained cooked or canned black beans

2 cups bean cooking liquid, or chicken, beef, or vegetable stock, store-bought broth, or water, preferably warmed

1 tablespoon ground cumin

Salt and freshly ground black pepper to taste

1 orange, well washed

1 pound Italian or other sausage, cut into 1-inch chunks

1 pound or more not-too-lean boneless pork (preferably from the shoulder), cut into 1-inch chunks

2 large onions, chopped

2 bell peppers, preferably red or yellow, stemmed, peeled if desired, seeded, and chopped

2 tablespoons minced garlic

1 cup dry red wine

1/2 cup orange juice, preferably freshly squeezed

Minced cilantro or fresh parsley leaves for garnish

1 Warm the beans in a large pot with the liquid; add the cumin, salt, and pepper. Peel the orange. Add the peel to the beans and section the flesh; set aside.

2 Turn the heat to medium under a large skillet. A minute later, add the sausage. Cook, turning occasionally, until browned on all sides; don't worry about it cooking through. Add to the beans.

3 Cook the pork bits in the same skillet, turning occasionally, until browned on all sides. Add to the beans.

4 Pour off all but about 3 tablespoons fat from the skillet. Add the onions and bell peppers and cook over medium heat, stirring occasionally, until the peppers soften, 8 to 10 minutes. Add the garlic and cook, stirring, 1 minute more. Add to the beans.

5 Turn the heat to high and add the red wine to the skillet. Cook, stirring and scraping to loosen any brown bits stuck to the bottom of the pan, until the wine is reduced by about half, about 5 minutes. Add to the beans, along with the orange juice. Taste the beans and season as necessary. Serve with rice, garnished with the reserved orange and some cilantro.

Black Beans and Rice, Spanish Style

This flavorful, filling black bean and white rice dish is commonly known as Moors and Christians. (The Muslim Moors ruled devoutly Christian Spain for seven centuries.) Make the rice ahead and use canned beans and this is one dish you'll prepare often. Although it won't be *quite* as attractive—none will provide the stark contrast of black on white—you can use any beans you like in this dish.

Makes 4 to 6 servings

Time: 30 minutes with precooked beans

2 tablespoons extra-virgin olive oil

1 medium onion, finely chopped

1 red or yellow bell pepper, stemmed, peeled if desired, and chopped

Salt and freshly ground black pepper to taste

1 tablespoon minced garlic

3 cups drained cooked or canned black beans

1 cup chopped tomatoes (canned are fine; don't bother to drain), optional

1 cup chicken, beef, or vegetable stock, store-bought broth, or water, preferably warmed

1/2 cup minced fresh parsley leaves

Rice Pilaf (page 84), or any of its variations

1 Place the oil in a large, deep skillet and turn the heat to medium. A minute later, add the onion and bell pepper. Season with salt and pepper and cook, stirring, until the bell pepper is soft, 8 to 10 minutes. Stir in the garlic, the beans, the optional tomatoes, and the liquid.

2 Turn the heat to medium-high and cook, stirring, until the beans are hot and most of the liquid is evaporated, 10 to 20 minutes. Stir in most of the parsley.

3 Arrange the pilaf on a platter, in a ring if you like. Spoon the beans over the rice or into the center of the ring, or pass them separately. Garnish with the remaining parsley and serve.

7 | Vegetables

Crisp-Cooked Asparagus   94

🕐 Braised Broccoli with Garlic and Wine   95

🕐 Quick-Braised Carrots with Butter   96

Chard with Pine Nuts and Currants   97

Grilled or Roasted Corn   98

🕐 Sautéed Mushrooms with Garlic   99

Pureed Parsnips   100

🕐 Buttered Peas   101

Sautéed Summer Squash or Zucchini   102

Microwaved or Simmered Sweet Potatoes   103

🕐 20 minutes or less

Crisp-Cooked Asparagus

Here you first simmer, steam, or microwave the asparagus, then quickly add nice taste and texture. Do not use pencil-thin asparagus for this recipe; you want a total of 20 to 25 fairly thick stalks.

Makes 4 servings

Time: 30 minutes

---

1 to 2 pounds asparagus, trimmed and peeled (below)

4 tablespoons (½ stick) butter or olive oil, or a combination

Flour for dredging

2 eggs, lightly beaten in a bowl

Plain bread crumbs

Lemon wedges

Preparing Asparagus

Snap off the bottom of each stalk; they will usually separate naturally right where the woody part ends.

All but the thinnest asparagus are best when peeled.

1 Simmer, steam, or microwave the asparagus; undercook it a little bit.

To simmer, lay them down in a skillet that can hold the spears without crowding, cover with salted water, cover the skillet, and turn the heat to high. Cook just until the thick part of the stalks can be pierced with a knife.

To steam, stand them up in a pot with an inch of salted water on the bottom (it's nice, but hardly essential, to tie them in a bundle first). Cover and turn the heat to high. Cook just until the thick part of the stalks can be pierced with a knife.

To microwave, lay them in a microwave-proof plate or shallow bowl with about 2 tablespoons of salted water; cover with a lid or plastic wrap. Microwave on high for 3 minutes, shake the container, and continue to microwave at 1-minute intervals, just until the thick part of the stalks can be pierced with a knife.

2 Drain and plunge asparagus into ice water, then drain and dry. (You may prepare the recipe in advance up to this point; refrigerate, well wrapped or in a covered container, for up to 2 days before proceeding.)

3 Heat the butter and/or oil in a large skillet over medium-high heat. When the butter foam subsides or the oil is hot, dredge each stalk lightly in the flour, dip it in the eggs, then dredge in the bread crumbs. Place in the pan. Repeat, turning the stalks as they brown and removing them as they finish. Cook in batches if necessary, keeping the finished stalks warm in a 200°F oven.

4 Serve hot, with lemon wedges.

Braised Broccoli with Garlic and Wine

A Roman preparation, great at room temperature, so it can be made in advance. You can use this technique for almost any vegetable—cauliflower, green beans—as needed. Anchovies add saltiness and richness to the dish. Leave them out entirely, or use less, if you like.

Makes 4 servings

Time: About 20 minutes

3 tablespoons olive oil

3 anchovies, minced (optional)

1 teaspoon minced garlic

About 1½ pounds broccoli, trimmed and cut up

1 cup dry white wine

Salt and freshly ground black pepper to taste

1 Place the oil in a large, deep skillet that can later be covered and turn the heat to medium. Add the anchovies and the garlic and cook, stirring occasionally, until the anchovies begin to break up and the garlic begins to color, 3 to 5 minutes.

2 Add the broccoli and cook, stirring, for 3 or 4 minutes. Add the wine and let it bubble away for a minute or two. Cover, turn the heat to medium-low, and cook for 2 or 3 minutes.

3 Uncover, return the heat to medium, and cook until most of the wine has evaporated and the broccoli is tender, about 5 minutes more. Season to taste (you will not need much salt) and serve hot or at room temperature.

Shopping Tip: Unless you know you hate them, anchovies are a great flavor booster. The best are sold packed in olive oil, and even if you buy a 1-pound jar you don't have to worry about them going bad after you open them. Simply keep the remainder submerged in oil (add more if you need to) and refrigerate; they will last indefinitely.

Quick-Braised Carrots with Butter

Best with butter, but also delicious when made with oil. For an even lighter touch, cut back on the oil (as below) and use it as a neutral cooking medium rather than as a flavor enhancer. Simply cooked carrots are good spiked with spices. In addition to ginger (see the variation), try ground cardamom, cinnamon, cumin, or coriander.

Makes 4 servings

Time: About 20 minutes

1 pound carrots, peeled and cut into ¼-inch-thick slices

2 tablespoons butter or 1 tablespoon canola or other neutral oil

¼ cup water

1 teaspoon sugar or 1 tablespoon maple syrup

Salt and freshly ground black pepper to taste

Minced fresh parsley, mint, chervil, or cilantro leaves for garnish

1 Place the carrots, butter or oil, water, sugar, salt, and pepper in a medium saucepan over high heat; bring to a boil and cover. Turn the heat to medium-low and cook for 5 minutes.

2 Uncover and raise the heat a bit. Cook, stirring occasionally, until the liquid has evaporated and the carrots are cooking in butter or oil. Lower the heat and continue to cook, stirring occasionally, until tender, a couple of minutes longer.

3 Taste and adjust the seasoning if necessary, then garnish and serve.

Quick-Braised Carrots with Orange and Ginger In Step 1, substitute ¼ cup orange juice (preferably freshly squeezed) and 1 tablespoon minced orange zest for the water. In Step 2, add 1 tablespoon peeled and minced fresh ginger to the saucepan after removing the cover. Step 3 remains the same.

Chard with Pine Nuts and Currants

This sweet dish, which is also great when made with spinach, is wonderful as an accompaniment to savory meats. Or thin it with a little more olive oil and some of the chard cooking water to make a good pasta sauce.

Makes 4 servings

Time: 30 minutes

2 pounds Swiss chard, washed and trimmed, leaves and stems separated, all roughly chopped

2 tablespoons olive oil

1/2 cup minced onion or shallot

1/2 cup pine nuts

1/2 cup currants (preferred) or raisins, soaked in warm water for about 10 minutes, drained

Salt and freshly ground black pepper to taste

1 Bring a large pot of water to a boil; salt it. Cook the stems of the Swiss chard until they are almost tender, about 5 minutes. Add the chopped leaves. Continue to cook until both stems and leaves are quite tender, another couple of minutes. Let the chard cool a bit, squeeze it dry, then chop it into smaller pieces.

2 As the chard is cooling, place the oil and onion or shallot in a large, deep skillet over medium heat. Cook (uncovered), stirring occasionally, until the onion or shallot is translucent, about 5 minutes.

3 Add the pine nuts and cook another minute, stirring, then add the chard, currants, and salt and pepper; cook, stirring, for about 2 minutes. Serve hot or at room temperature.

Shopping Tip: Essentially a beet grown for leaves rather than roots, chard has a thick midrib which is white, pink, or brilliant red; the leaves are sometimes ruffled and are deep green, green with rich scarlet veins, or dark reddish-purple (there is also rainbow chard, with a variety of colors). Chard has a distinctive, acid-sweet flavor that makes it unlike any other vegetable; most people like the taste.

Grilled or Roasted Corn

Although steamed corn-on-the-cob is standard, grilled corn is the ultimate. Slightly charred kernels are crispy-sweet; here, a little blackening is a good thing. If you prefer more moist, less crisp corn, leave the husks on when you grill them. Some people also soak the corn, in the husks, to reduce burning.

Makes 4 servings

Time: 20 minutes, plus time to preheat the grill

8 ears fresh corn

Salt and freshly ground black pepper to taste

Butter (optional)

Preparing Corn

The "silk" must always be removed from corn before cooking. You can remove the husk, or simply peel it back and take out the silk, then fold the husk back over the corn. This works well for grilling; for steaming or boiling, remove the husk entirely.

Use a sharp knife to scrape kernels from the cob.

1 Start a charcoal or wood fire, or preheat a gas grill, or turn the oven to 450°F. Peel back, but don't remove, the husks of the corn and remove the inner silks (see illustration, at left). Smooth the husks back in place, but don't worry about them completely covering the kernels. Or, if you prefer, shuck the corn entirely.

2 Grill or roast the corn, turning occasionally. With husks on, timing will be 15 to 20 minutes on the grill, 20 to 30 minutes in the oven. With husks off, less than half those times will be needed. When some of the kernels char a bit and others are lightly browned, the corn is done. Serve with salt, pepper, and butter.

Garlicky or Spicy Grilled or Roasted Corn For a flavorful twist, brush the corn with Garlic Butter (page 51) or Chile Oil (page 51) before roasting (or before re-closing the husks around the corn).

Sautéed Mushrooms with Garlic

These are best served at room temperature but are, of course, delicious freshly cooked. Stir in some other herbs—such as chives, chervil, and/or tarragon—and a teaspoon or two of good vinegar along with the parsley if you like.

Makes 4 servings

Time: About 20 minutes

½ cup extra-virgin olive oil

About 1 pound mushrooms, preferably an assortment, cleaned, trimmed, and sliced; mix in some reconstituted dried mushrooms for extra flavor if you like (See Mushroom Varieties, at right)

Salt and freshly ground black pepper to taste

¼ cup dry white wine

1 teaspoon minced garlic

2 tablespoons chopped fresh parsley leaves

1 Place the olive oil in a large, deep skillet over medium heat. When it is hot, add the mushrooms, then some salt and pepper. Cook, stirring occasionally, until tender, 10 to 15 minutes.

2 Add the wine and let it bubble away for just 1 minute or so longer. Turn the heat to low. Add the garlic and parsley, stir, and cook for 1 minute. Turn off the heat. Serve hot or allow the mushrooms to sit in this mixture for a few minutes (up to 1 hour, if you have time) before serving.

Mushroom Varieties

Button: The common white-to-tan cultivated mushroom. Much improved when cooked with some reconstituted dried porcini, or with some fresh shiitakes.

Cremini/Portobello: The second is merely a giant version of the first. Both are domesticated brown mushrooms, and have much better flavor than button mushrooms. Portobellos are wonderful grilled.

Chanterelle: Wild and domesticated, a good, fleshy mushroom with subtle flavor.

Oyster: Wild and domesticated, a good choice in supermarkets. Great sautéed, and especially quick-cooking.

Morel: Fine-flavored and odd-textured. Found wild all over the North, and sometimes in a large enough quantity to make it to stores (although rarely supermarkets). Sold dried.

Porcini (Cèpes): Meaty and spectacular. Buy from a reputable dealer in quantities of at least an ounce at a time; the small packages of ⅛-ounce for $3 are among the world's greatest rip-offs.

Shiitake: The best domesticated mushroom, now sold in most supermarkets. Great flavor. Also sold dried (the Chinese black mushroom is shiitake and is usually very inexpensive). The stem is too tough to be eaten; discard or use it in stocks.

Pureed Parsnips

The parsnip is probably the best vegetable that never gets eaten. Parsnips are sweeter than even carrots, easy to prepare, and they have great shelf life—you can store them like carrots, for weeks or even months. Their most common and best use is pureed, but they are also wonderful mixed with other vegetables in a roasting pan or cooked in any way you would carrots.

Parsnips can be combined with soft-cooked potatoes, turnips, or carrots before pureeing. Because they have a tendency to become waterlogged, it's best to steam or microwave parsnips rather than boil them.

Makes 4 servings

Time: 30 minutes

About 1½ pounds parsnips, peeled, cored if necessary, cut into chunks

Salt and freshly ground black pepper to taste

2 tablespoons butter

2 tablespoons cream, milk, or reserved parsnip cooking water, as needed

¼ cup minced fresh parsley leaves, plus more for garnish

1 **To steam the parsnips,** place them in a steamer above an inch or two of salted water. Cover and cook about 15 minutes, or until they can be easily pierced with a thin-bladed knife. Drain.

To microwave them, place the parsnips in a microwave-proof plate or shallow bowl with about 2 tablespoons of salted water; cover with a lid or plastic wrap. Microwave on high for 6 minutes, shake the container, and continue to microwave at 2-minute intervals, until the parsnips can be easily pierced with a thin-bladed knife. Drain.

2 Place the parsnips in the container of a food processor along with salt, pepper, and butter. Puree, adding the liquid of your choice through the feed tube, until the mixture is smooth and creamy but not too thin. (You may prepare the recipe in advance up to this point; refrigerate, well wrapped or in a covered container, for up to 2 days before proceeding.) Place in a bowl or small saucepan.

3 Stir in the ¼ cup parsley, then taste and adjust seasoning. Reheat over very low heat, stirring almost constantly, or in the microwave. Garnish and serve.

Shopping Tip: The best season for parsnips is fall, but you can usually find them year-round. You want relatively small ones, 4 to 6 per pound. Avoid soft or flabby specimens.

Preparation Tip: Treat parsnips as you would a carrot. If the parsnip is large (more than 1 inch thick at its broad end), you must remove its woody core: Cut the thinner portion off and set it aside. Cut the thick portion in half and dig out the core with the end of a vegetable peeler, a paring knife, or a sharp spoon; the procedure is neither difficult nor time-consuming.

Buttered Peas

It's tough to shell enough fresh peas to cook in any quantity, since the temptation to eat while you shell is overwhelming. But should you have 2 cups or so (you need at least 1 1/2 pounds of unshelled peas in pods), cook them this way, which is also the best way to cook frozen peas.

Makes 4 servings

Time: 15 minutes

2 cups shelled fresh peas or frozen peas

1 to 2 tablespoons butter

Salt and freshly ground black pepper to taste

2 tablespoons minced fresh mint, basil, chervil, or parsley leaves (optional)

1 Bring a small pot of water to the boil over high heat; salt it. Place the peas in it, with the heat still on high, and cook for 2 to 3 minutes, no more—just until the peas are bright green and tender.

2 Drain the peas. Place the butter in a medium-to-large skillet and turn the heat to medium. When the butter melts, turn the heat to low and cook the peas, salt and pepper, and optional herb in it for 2 or 3 minutes, shaking the skillet occasionally, just until the peas are hot and coated with butter.

Shopping Tip: To buy peas to shell, open a pod or two in the store; they should be full of medium-sized peas. Big peas can be tough, so taste a couple; if you want to keep eating, buy them. If the peas are large and tough, they will need to be cooked before eating.

Preparation Tips: Store all peas, loosely wrapped in plastic, in the vegetable bin. But use them quickly; their sweetness is fleeting.

With the flat end of the pea down, grasp the tip of the flower end and pull down, removing the string along the bottom of the pea.

Sautéed Summer Squash or Zucchini

Salting grated summer squash enables you to brown it quickly, but it isn't essential; let it rest for up to 30 minutes if you have time, but skip the step entirely if you do not.

Makes 4 servings

Time: 15 to 30 minutes

About 2 pounds summer squash or zucchini, the smaller the better

1 tablespoon salt (optional)

3 to 4 tablespoons olive or other oil

1 clove garlic, smashed (optional)

Freshly ground black pepper to taste

Minced fresh mint, parsley, or basil leaves for garnish

1 Coarsely grate the squash by hand or with the grating disk of a food processor. If time allows, place grated squash in a colander and salt it liberally—use 1 tablespoon or more of salt. Toss to blend and let drain 15 to 30 minutes. Rinse quickly and dry by wringing in a towel.

2 When you're ready to cook, place the oil in a large non-stick skillet and turn the heat to medium-high; add the garlic if you choose to do so. When the oil is hot, toss the squash in the oil, sprinkle with pepper, and raise the heat to high. Cook, stirring frequently, until the squash is browned, about 10 minutes. Garnish and serve hot.

Microwaved or Simmered Sweet Potatoes

Flavorful, satisfying, simple. What more could you ask for? This also works perfectly for any winter squash, such as butternut or acorn squash. If you like your sweetness balanced with some acidity, add a little lemon juice to this mix.

Makes 4 servings

Time: About 20 to 30 minutes

2 pounds sweet potatoes, peeled and cut into chunks

2 tablespoons butter or canola or other neutral oil

2 tablespoons maple syrup or brown sugar

1 tablespoon freshly squeezed lemon juice (optional)

Salt and freshly ground black pepper to taste

To microwave, combine all ingredients with 2 tablespoons of water in a microwave-proof plate or shallow bowl; cover with a lid or plastic wrap. Microwave on high for 3 minutes, shake the container, and continue to microwave at 2-minute intervals, until the sweet potatoes are very tender. Serve hot.

To simmer, combine all ingredients with $1/3$ cup of water in a covered saucepan, turn the heat to medium, and bring to a boil. Turn the heat to low and cook, stirring every 5 minutes or so and adding a little additional water if necessary, until the sweet potatoes are very tender, 20 to 30 minutes. Serve hot.

8 | Desserts

Sautéed Apples   106

🕐 Raspberry Fool   107

🕐 Strawberries with Balsamic Vinegar   108

Easy Waffles with Ice Cream   109

   🕐 Hot Fudge   109

Oatmeal Cookies   110

Chocolate Mousse   111

🕐 20 minutes or less

Sautéed Apples

The only challenge to this recipe is that it must be cooked at the last minute. Serve as is or with a scoop of vanilla ice cream or a dollop of whipped cream.

Makes 4 servings

Time: 30 minutes

4 tablespoons (½ stick) unsalted butter

About 1½ pounds firm crisp apples, such as Golden Delicious, peeled, cored, and cut into 8 or 10 pieces each

½ cup white or brown sugar

½ teaspoon ground cinnamon

1 Place the butter in a large, deep skillet and turn the heat to medium. When the butter melts, add the apples and stir; turn the heat to low, cover, and cook for 10 minutes.

2 Add the sugar and cinnamon and raise the heat to medium. Cook, stirring frequently, until the apples are tender and glazed, another 10 minutes or so. Serve hot or warm.

Sautéed Bananas Start with 4 bananas, ripe but not too soft, and peel them, then cut them in half crosswise, then lengthwise, so that each banana has been divided into 4 pieces. Dredge them lightly in flour, then cook in butter as above, turning only once, after the first side has browned, about 5 minutes. Reduce the (white) sugar to about 2 tablespoons, and omit the cinnamon. Serve, passing additional sugar at the table.

Raspberry Fool

A perfect treatment for raspberries, which require no cooking at all to be tender. But a fool—pureed cooked fruit blended with whipped cream—can be made with any fruit: Just toss with cream and sugar to taste. (For stone fruit, pit, peel, and chop first.) Superfine sugar—or second-choice, confectioners' sugar—blends better than granulated sugar.

Makes 4 to 6 servings

Time: 20 minutes

2 to 3 cups fresh raspberries

1/2 cup superfine or confectioners' sugar, plus 1 tablespoon, or more if needed, for the cream

1 cup heavy cream, preferably not ultra-pasteurized

1 Puree about one-third of the raspberries in a blender with 1/4 cup sugar. Force the puree through a sieve (or fine-meshed strainer) to remove seeds. Taste; the puree should be quite sweet. If it is not, add a little more sugar.

2 Toss the remaining berries with 1/4 cup sugar. With an electric mixer or a wire whisk beat the cream with 1 tablespoon sugar, until it holds soft peaks. Beat in the raspberry puree, then fold in the sugared berries. Taste and add more sugar if necessary. Serve immediately or refrigerate for up to an hour.

Strawberries with Balsamic Vinegar

If you've never had this, try it. In the Italian region in which *aceto balsamico* originated, drizzling the real stuff over berries is common. True balsamic has a mellowed flavor; it's not as acidic as lesser-quality balsamic vinegar. A tiny sprinkling of black pepper is quite nice here, too.

Makes 4 to 6 servings

Time: 10 minutes

1 quart strawberries, washed, hulled, and sliced

1/4 cup sugar, or more to taste

1 tablespoon high-quality balsamic vinegar, or more to taste

About 1/8 teaspoon freshly ground black pepper

1 Toss the strawberries with the 1/4 cup sugar and let sit for 10 minutes.

2 Sprinkle with the vinegar; taste and add more sugar or vinegar if necessary. Sprinkle with the pepper and serve.

Shopping Tip: The ideal balsamic is the thirty-year-old, $100 kind, which is hardly practical. But there are alternatives, in the way of "halfway" balsamic vinegars, which are aged for up to three years and cost about $10 per half-liter. This is not cheap, but if you find a brand that has good, "warm" flavor, stick with it and you will be satisfied; you won't use it up that fast.

Preparation Tip: If all you can find is the common $4 (per half-liter) bottle of balsamic vinegar, it can be made to work: Reduce about 1/4 cup of it over high heat (in a very small saucepan, to prevent burning) to about 1 tablespoon. It becomes syrupy and surprisingly sweet.

Easy Waffles with Ice Cream

Waffles are a treat for breakfast but they are also a quick dessert foundation—simply top them with ice cream, and hot fudge, if you like. If you have the time, separate the eggs and beat the whites for a lighter texture, or try some of the flavor variations.

Makes 4 to 6 servings

Time: 20 to 30 minutes

Canola or other neutral oil for brushing on waffle iron

2 cups all-purpose flour

$\frac{1}{2}$ teaspoon salt

2 tablespoons sugar

3 teaspoons baking powder

1$\frac{1}{2}$ cups milk

2 eggs

4 tablespoons ($\frac{1}{2}$ stick) butter, melted and cooled

1 teaspoon vanilla extract (optional)

4 to 6 scoops vanilla or other ice cream

4 to 6 tablespoons (or more) Hot Fudge, optional (at right)

3 Quick Variations for Waffles

1 Substitute 1 cup cornmeal for 1 cup flour. It's really worth separating the eggs and beating the whites in this instance.

2 Stir 1 cup chopped (not minced) nuts or shredded sweetened or unsweetened coconut into the batter.

3 Add minced or grated orange or lemon zest, about 2 teaspoons per batch of batter.

1 Brush the waffle iron lightly with oil and preheat it.

2 Combine the dry ingredients. Mix together the milk and eggs. Stir in the butter and vanilla (if you are using it). Stir the wet mixture into the dry ingredients. If the mixture seems too thick to pour, add a little more milk.

3 Spread a ladleful or so of batter onto the waffle iron. After 2 minutes, gently pull up on the top of the iron. If there is resistance, let cook another minute or two longer. (It usually takes about 3 to 5 minutes.) Serve immediately, with a scoop of ice cream and hot fudge, if desired, or keep warm for a few minutes in a low oven and add toppings before serving.

Hot Fudge

Makes about 1$\frac{1}{2}$ cups • Time: 15 minutes

You can buy hot fudge, but it's quick and fun to make. This is chewy and fudgy when you put it on top of ice cream.

4 ounces semisweet or bittersweet chocolate, chopped

4 tablespoons ($\frac{1}{2}$ stick) unsalted butter

$\frac{1}{4}$ cup sugar

Pinch salt

$\frac{1}{4}$ cup water

$\frac{1}{3}$ cup light corn syrup

1 teaspoon vanilla extract

1 Combine all ingredients except corn syrup and vanilla in a small saucepan over very low heat. Cook, stirring, until the chocolate melts and the mixture is smooth. Add the corn syrup. Bring to a boil, turn the heat to low, and cook for 5 to 10 minutes, until thick and shiny.

2 Add the vanilla and serve immediately, or keep warm over hot water until ready to serve, or refrigerate for up to a week and reheat very gently (a double boiler is best) before using.

Oatmeal Cookies

These are good—anytime. They can be made with raisins, chopped dried fruit (cranberries and cherries are good), chocolate chips, or coconut—the batter can handle up to 1½ cups of any of these, or a combination. Stir them into the batter along with the dry ingredients.

Makes 3 to 4 dozen

Time: About 30 minutes

8 tablespoons (1 stick) unsalted butter, softened

½ cup white sugar

½ cup brown sugar

2 eggs

1½ cups (about 7 ounces) all-purpose flour

2 cups rolled oats (not the instant kind)

½ teaspoon ground cinnamon

Pinch salt

2 teaspoons baking powder

½ cup milk

½ teaspoon vanilla or almond extract

1 Preheat the oven to 375°F.

2 Use an electric mixer to cream together the butter and sugars; add the eggs one at a time and beat until well blended.

3 Combine the flour, oats, cinnamon, salt, and baking powder in a bowl. Alternating with the milk, add the dry ingredients to the batter by hand, a little a time, stirring to blend. Stir in the vanilla or almond extract. Drop by teaspoons or tablespoons onto ungreased baking sheets and bake until lightly browned, 12 to 15 minutes.

4 Cool for about 2 minutes on the sheets before using a spatula to transfer the cookies to a rack to finish cooling. Serve or store in a covered container at room temperature for no more than a day or two.

Lacy Oatmeal Cookies Melt the butter and combine it with the sugars, oats, and salt; beat in the eggs. Omit the flour, baking powder, milk, and vanilla; add the cinnamon if you like. Bake at 350°F on greased baking sheets for 8 to 10 minutes; let rest a minute before removing with a thin-bladed spatula. Cool on a rack.

Chocolate Mousse

Once thought of as the most elegant of desserts, this ultra-rich chocolate pudding is still a real winner. Strictly speaking, the chilling time makes it take longer than 30 minutes, but if you make it before you begin cooking, and serve it after you're done eating, it will be perfect, and the preparation time is very quick. Once the chocolate is melted, the cooking is over; the mousse just sits until it sets up.

You can spike chocolate mousse with rum, coffee, or other flavorings, but I like it simple—it's the intensity of chocolate that makes it special.

Makes 6 servings

Time: 20 minutes, plus time to chill

---

2 tablespoons unsalted butter

4 ounces bittersweet or semisweet chocolate, chopped

3 eggs, separated

1/4 cup sugar

1/2 cup heavy cream

1/2 teaspoon vanilla extract

1 Use a double boiler or a small saucepan over low heat to melt the butter and chocolate together. Just before the chocolate finishes melting, remove it from the stove and beat with a wooden spoon until smooth.

2 Transfer the chocolate mixture to a bowl and beat in the egg yolks with a whisk. Refrigerate.

3 Beat the egg whites with half the sugar until they hold stiff peaks but are not dry. Set aside. Beat the cream with the remaining sugar and vanilla until it holds soft peaks.

4 Stir a couple of spoonfuls of the whites into the chocolate mixture to lighten it a bit, then fold in the remaining whites thoroughly but gently. Fold in the cream and refrigerate until chilled. If you are in a hurry, divide the mousse among 6 cups; it will chill much faster. Serve within a day or two of making.

Quick Menus

Quick Italian Dinner

Penne with Ricotta, Parmesan, and Peas	p. 23
🌙 Tuscan Steak	p. 65
🌙 Braised Broccoli with Garlic and Wine	p. 95

Quick Italian Lunch

Sautéed Italian Sausage with Peppers and Onions	p. 71
Chard with Pine Nuts and Currants	p. 97

Quick Asian Dinner

🌙 Cabbage and Carrot Salad with Soy-Lime Dressing	p. 4
Crisp Pan-Fried Noodle Cake	p. 31
Stir-Fried Spicy Beef with Basil	p. 68

Quick Asian Lunch

Stir-Fried Beef with Onions	p. 67
🌙 Fried Rice with Greens	p. 86

Quick Mexican Lunch

Bean Burritos with Meat	p. 81
🌙 Twice-Cooked ("Refried") Beans with Cumin	p. 88

Quick Mediterranean Lunch

Lamburgers with Smoked Mozzarella	p. 80
Chickpeas with Lemon	p. 87

Quick Vegetarian Lunch

🌙 Simple Greek Salad	p. 2
Corn, Tomato, and Zucchini Soup with Basil	p. 12

Quick Vegetarian Dinner

Mushroom Soup (with vegetable broth)	p. 10
Bean and Tomato Casserole	p. 89

Quick Low-Carbohydrate Dinner

Herb Frittata	p. 8
🌙 Salmon Roasted in Butter	p. 42
🌙 Raspberry Fool	p. 107

Quick Summer Dinner

Broiled or Grilled Chicken with Pesto	p. 50
Grilled or Roasted Corn	p. 98
🌙 Raspberry Fool	p. 107

Quick Fall Dinner

Herb-Roasted Chicken Cutlets	p. 54
Pureed Parsnips	p. 100

Quick Anytime Dinner

🌙 Cheese Quesadillas	p. 9
Sautéed Summer Squash or Zucchini	p. 102

Quick Weeknight Family Dinner

Sautéed Pork Chops	p. 72
🌙 Quick-Braised Carrots with Butter	p. 96
🌙 Buttered Peas	p. 101
Easy Waffles with Ice Cream	p. 109

Quick Weekend Family Dinner

Quick Chicken Soup with Rice or Noodles	p. 14
Red Snapper or Other Fillets in Packages with Spinach	p. 39
Black Beans and Rice, Spanish Style	p. 91
Oatmeal Cookies	p. 110

Quick Elegant Lunch

Warm Salad of Scallops and
   Tender Greens   p. 47
Rice Pilaf   p. 84

Quick Brunch

Great Green Salad   p. 2
Vinaigrette/Quick Blue Cheese Dressing   p. 3
Vegetable Frittata   p. 8
Sautéed Apples   p. 106
Easy Waffles with Ice Cream   p. 109

Quick Casual Dinner Party

Cabbage and Carrot Salad with
   Soy-Lime Dressing   p. 4
Greens with Bacon   p. 5
Chicken Satay   p. 57
Strawberries with Balsamic Vinegar   p. 108

Quick Elegant Dinner Party

Roast Rack of Lamb with Persillade   p. 79
Rice Pilaf   p. 84
Crisp-Cooked Asparagus   p. 94
Chocolate Mousse   p. 111

Recipes That Take 20 Minutes (or Less)

Starters

Great Green Salad	p. 2
Simple Greek Salad	p. 2
Arugula and Blue Cheese Salad	p. 2
Vinaigrette	p. 3
Quick Blue Cheese Dressing	p. 3
Cabbage and Carrot Salad with Soy-Lime Dressing	p. 4
Omelet	p. 6
Mushroom Omelet	p. 7
Spanish Omelet	p. 7
Western Omelet	p. 7
Cheese Quesadillas	p. 9
Lightning-Quick Fish Soup	p. 15

Pasta

Pasta with Tomato Sauce	p. 18

Fish

Broiled Flatfish or Other Thin White Fillets	p. 34
Broiled Flatfish or Other Thin White Fillets with Mustard and Herbs	p. 35
Broiled Flatfish or Other Thin White Fillets with Garlic-Parsley Sauce	p. 35
Sautéed Flatfish or Other Thin White Fillets	p. 36
Sautéed Flatfish or Other Thin White Fillets with Curry and Lime	p. 37
Sautéed Flatfish or Other Thin White Fillets with Soy Sauce	p. 37
Sautéed Flatfish or Other Thin White Fillets with Sesame Crust	p. 37
Sautéed Cod or Other Thick White Fillets	p. 38
Extra-Crisp Sautéed Cod or Other Thick White Fillets	p. 38

Salmon Roasted in Butter	p. 42
Salmon Roasted with Herbs	p. 42
Salmon Roasted with Buttered Almonds	p. 42
Shrimp "Marinara"	p. 44
Shrimp with Feta Cheese	p. 44
Sautéed Scallops	p. 46
Buttery Scallops	p. 46
Ginger Scallops	p. 46
Warm Salad of Scallops and Tender Greens	p. 47

Poultry

Pesto	p. 51
Garlic Butter	p. 51
Chile Oil	p. 51
Sautéed Chicken Cutlets	p. 52
Spice-Coated Chicken Cutlets	p. 52
Sesame-Coated Chicken Cutlets	p. 52
Crunchy Curried Chicken Breasts	p. 55

Meat

Broiled Steak	p. 65
Pan-Grilled Steak	p. 65
Tuscan Steak	p. 65
Pan-Seared Steak with Red Wine Sauce	p. 66
Stir-Fried Pork with Spinach	p. 74
Stir-Fried Pork with Sweet Onions	p. 75
Stir-Fried Pork with Snow Peas and Ginger	p. 75
Sautéed Medallions of Pork with Lemon and Parsley	p. 76
Lamb Medallions with Shallots, Tarragon, and Red Wine	p. 78
Tomato-Onion Salsa	p. 81

Rice and Beans

Fried Rice with Greens	p. 86
Toasted Sesame Seeds	p. 86
Twice-Cooked ("Refried") Beans with Cumin	p. 88
Traditional Refried Beans	p. 88

Vegetables

Braised Broccoli with Garlic and Wine	p. 95
Quick-Braised Carrots with Butter	p. 96
Quick-Braised Carrots with Orange and Ginger	p. 96
Sautéed Mushrooms with Garlic	p. 99
Buttered Peas	p. 101

Desserts

Raspberry Fool	p. 107
Strawberries with Balsamic Vinegar	p. 108
Hot Fudge	p. 109

Tips Reference

Here's an at-a-glance reference of the tips in this book. If you're ever looking for some quick info—on "steak," for example—you can look here, instead of scanning the index and flipping through recipe pages trying to find it. The page reference leads you back to the related recipe, if you want to consult it.

Anchovies	Unless you know you hate them, anchovies are a great flavor booster. The best are sold packed in olive oil, and even if you buy a 1-pound jar you don't have to worry about them going bad after you open them. Simply keep the remainder submerged in oil (add more if you need to) and refrigerate; they will last indefinitely. *See page 95.*
Bacon	Slab bacon is not only usually of higher quality than presliced bacon, it keeps longer, and it can be cut into chunks, a desirable option for flavor and texture in some dishes. *See page 5.*
Balsamic vinegar	The ideal balsamic is the thirty-year-old, $100 kind, which is hardly practical. But there are alternatives, in the way of "halfway" balsamic vinegars, which are aged for up to three years and cost about $10 per half-liter. This is not cheap, but if you find a brand that has good, "warm" flavor, stick with it and you will be satisfied; you won't use it up that fast. *See page 108.*
	If all you can find is the common $4 (per half-liter) bottle of balsamic vinegar, it can be made to work: Reduce about ¼ cup of it over high heat (in a very small saucepan, to prevent burning) to about 1 tablespoon. It becomes syrupy and surprisingly sweet. *See page 108*
Beef	You can grill the beef well ahead of time and slice it at the last minute. All beef (and most meat) slices more easily, and retains more of its juice, if you let it rest for a little while—5 to 10 minutes—before carving. *See page 69.*
Fermented black beans	Fermented black beans are sold in every Chinese market and, because they are packed with loads of salt, keep indefinitely (unrefrigerated). Use them sparingly, as they are very strongly flavored. *See page 59.*
Broth	Most canned broths are weak. Still, they're usually more flavorful than water (which is still a decent alternative). Generally, buy "low-sodium" varieties and avoid those containing MSG. Broths sold in boxes are a slightly better option because they don't have as much of the off flavors associated with canned foods. *See page 14.*
Chard	Essentially a beet grown for leaves rather than roots, chard has a thick midrib, which is white, pink, or brilliant red; the leaves are sometimes ruffled and are deep green, green with rich scarlet veins, or dark reddish-purple (there is also rainbow chard, with a variety of colors). Chard has a distinctive, acid-sweet flavor that makes it unlike any other vegetable; most people like the taste. *See page 97.*
Creamy blue cheese	Use good-quality Gorgonzola or substitute another creamy blue cheese, such as Roquefort (from France—made from sheep's milk and especially delicious), or Stilton (from England). Try to avoid domestic blue cheeses, unless you can find a really special one, like Maytag blue. *See page 21.*
Chicken	Start with a high-quality chicken, preferably free-range chicken or Kosher (unfortunately, the word "natural" doesn't mean much). Either of these will have more flavor than commercial chickens, though they'll also be somewhat more expensive. *See page 50.*

Chicken	Cook chicken quickly, use cut-up chicken, or cut it up yourself. Be sure to separate the leg and thigh; that joint (easy to find, and easy to cut through) is the slowest cooking part of the bird if you leave it intact. *See page 50.*
	Overcooking boneless breasts—the most popular cut—is a real problem. Generally speaking, 6 minutes—3 per side—is sufficient time to cook a thin piece of chicken breast; 10 minutes will do for a plump piece. When it's done, the inside will be moist and a tiny bit pink, not dry and stark white. *See page 53.*
	Because they are as close to a blank canvas as exists in food, chicken breasts showcase other flavors very, very well. Fresh herbs—especially tarragon, chervil, parsley, or other assertive but slightly sweet herbs—are ideal; dried herbs work well, too, but should be used in small doses as they quickly become overwhelming. *See page 54.*
	Chicken wings have two joints; simply cut between them to create three pieces from each wing. The outermost tip should be saved for stock, as it has virtually no meat on it. *See page 59.*
	You can usually find boneless chicken thighs in the supermarket, but if you cannot, and you don't wish to bone them yourself (it's intuitive, and quite simple), substitute boneless breasts. *See page 60.*
Chickpeas	For flavor or bulk, you can add cooked, crumbled ground meat, or a handful or two of good croutons to the simply cooked chickpeas. *See page 87.*
Clams	The biggest and toughest clams are chopped into bits to be made into chowder. The choicest—essentially the smallest—are sold live, and are great raw, on the half-shell. In recent years we have seen more and more cockles—very small clams—in our markets, and they are the best for Linguine with Clams. *See page 29.*
	Buying clams is easy, because those in the shell must be alive. You'd know when hard-shells have died; the shells separate easily. Otherwise, they're shut up pretty tight, and you cannot even slide their shells from side to side. Dead clams smell pretty bad, so it's unlikely you'll be fooled. *See page 29.*
	Never store clams in sealed plastic or under water; they'll die. Just keep them in a bowl in the refrigerator, where they will remain alive for several days. *See page 29.*
	Hard-shell clams require little more than a cleaning of their shells. I use a stiff brush to scrub them under running water. *See page 29.*
Curry powder	As most experienced cooks know, curry powder is not a spice but a blend of spices (in India the related seasoning mix is called garam masala). You can make it yourself, to taste, but few non-Indians ever get to that point. Try to find a brand you like, and buy it fresh, replacing it about once a year even if it isn't used up; like all spices, it loses potency over time. *See page 55.*
	Curry powder is a spice blend that includes cumin, black pepper, and ground chile powder, among other spices, including turmeric, which gives it its yellow color; garam masala is a brown spice blend with a spicy-sweet edge from ground cinnamon, cardamom, and cloves. Look for them in Indian and Asian markets, although now they can often be found in supermarkets. Try different brands to find your preferred blend. *See page 61.*

Fish   If you're buying fish, especially for fish soup, look for sturdy, white-fleshed varieties like red snapper, monkfish, or grouper. Oily fish like salmon is too rich for soups, and delicate fish like flounder simply falls apart. Of course, shellfish—clams, mussels, shrimp, and so on—are perfect additions. *See page 15.*

Thin fish fillets cook very, very quickly and overcook almost as fast. A ¼-inch-thick flounder fillet can, under the right circumstances, cook through in 2 minutes. Even a relatively thick piece of red snapper will be done in less than 10 minutes in almost every instance. *See page 34.*

I usually don't bother to heat plates, but thin fish fillets cool off so quickly that it's worth it in this instance. If you don't want to turn on the oven, run the plates under steaming hot water for a minute, then dry. *See page 36.*

If you use a non-stick skillet, you can turn a fish fillet—even one cooked in a minimum of fat—without much trouble. Make sure to turn it before it is fully cooked, however, or it may fall apart. Try turning after just 2 minutes of cooking. *See page 36.*

Some of the thick fish fillet choices are from the same fish as some thin fillets (they're simply cut from larger fish), and some from fish that produce only thick fillets. In any case, they're all white, tender, and mild-flavored, at least an inch thick (and usually considerably thicker than that—1½ inches is common, and 2 inches not unheard of). *See page 38.*

Greens   Any greens, as long as they're tender enough, can be used in salads. If you were to pick only one, romaine makes the most sense: It's got both tender and crunchy parts, and it is slightly but not too bitter. These days, you can buy "mesclun" assortments either in bulk or in packages, in almost every supermarket. They're colorful, flavorful, often organic, and usually quite fresh; the only downside is that they tend to be expensive. *See page 2.*

Herbs   Almost any herb will be delicious with cooked rice, so it's a good place to experiment. If you can find chervil, a fragile herb that is not often sold in supermarkets, you'll be surprised at how delicious it is. Shiso, an herb popular in Mexico (where it's called *perilla*) and Japan (where it's served with sushi), is another good choice. But parsley, mint, or cilantro is also great with rice. *See page 85.*

Fresh tarragon is delicious, but it's also one of the few herbs that dries well. Use just a pinch of dried tarragon, crumbled between your fingers, in place of a sprig. Other herbs that are good with Red Snapper are fresh thyme (again, a sprig, or use a pinch of dried), or fresh basil (a few leaves per piece of fish), parsley (a sprig or two per piece), or chervil (again, a sprig or two per piece)—the dried versions of these last herbs are useless. *See page 39.*

Kale and collards   Kale and collards—its flat-leaved relative—are interchangeable. Cooking time for either will be considerably shorter if you avoid thick stems; usually those with ¼-inch-thick stems are easier to cook and to eat. *See page 11.*

Lamb   If you take a rack of lamb and cut it up, you get *lamb rib chops,* which are the most tender and least fatty. *Loin chops* are similar. Both rib and loin chops should be cooked rare to medium-rare. The far less expensive *shoulder chops,* however, are equally flavorful; you just have to discard a bit more gristle and fat and do a bit more chewing. In addition, they're better cooked a little longer, until just about medium. *See page 77.*

Lamb	Keep in mind that in a rack of lamb there are seven ribs per rack, and only a couple of bites per rib. You'll need two racks for four people, although, the fourteen ribs could serve five people in a pinch, and even six if there's plenty of other food and the crowd isn't ravenous. *See page 79.*

Make sure the chine bone (backbone) is removed from the rack of lamb so you can easily cut through the ribs to separate them at the table, but don't bother to ask to have the ribs "frenched" (the meat removed from the top of the bones); the crisp meat along the bones is one of the pleasures of a rack of lamb. *See page 79.*

Ground lamb can be cooked longer than ground beef without suffering from dryness and toughness, but it should still be left somewhat pink inside. *See page 80.*

Mushrooms

Store fresh mushrooms, loosely wrapped in waxed paper (not plastic), in the refrigerator bin; they often keep upward of a week. *See page 10.*

Rinse mushrooms as lightly as you can (they absorb water like a sponge if they sit in it), but make sure to get dirt out of hidden crevices; with some mushrooms, it's easier to trim them first. Cut off any hard or dried-out spots—usually just the end of the stem. The stems of most mushrooms are perfectly edible, but those of shiitake should be discarded or reserved for stock. *See page 10.*

Nam pla

Nam pla—Thai fish sauce, called *nuoc mam* in Vietnam—is little more than fish, salt, and water, and an ancient way of preserving fish and adding its flavor to foods long after the catch is made. It's strong-flavored (and even stronger-smelling) but a great and distinctive substitute for soy sauce. *See page 68.*

Omelets

Once, omelets were difficult to make, and required a lot of fat to keep from sticking. The non-stick pan changed that. With it, you can make an omelet successfully, on the first try, with a minimum of fat. If you want to make omelets for one, get a 6- or 8-inch skillet; for larger omelets, use a 10- or 12-inch skillet. *See page 6.*

Pancetta

Pancetta is cured—that is, salted—unsmoked bacon. It's available at good Italian markets. Buy ¼-inch-thick slices, and freeze them individually; you don't even have to thaw them before using in recipes. *See page 24.*

Parmesan cheese

You cannot substitute for freshly grated cheese, and real Parmesan—among the world's greatest cheeses from the area around Parma—is now sold everywhere. It can be expensive, but it lasts a long time (unless you start nibbling on it, which is understandable). *See page 23.*

Look for the brown rind with "Parmigiano-Reggiano" stenciled on it. Everything else called "Parmesan" cheese is an imitation, although some of the imitations (like Grana Padano) are decent; hard sheep's cheese ("pecorino Romano," for example) is stronger but a decent substitute on strong-flavored dishes. *See page 23.*

Parsnips

The best season for parsnips is fall, but you can usually find them year-round. You want relatively small ones, 4 to 6 per pound. Avoid soft or flabby specimens. *See page 100.*

Parsnips Treat parsnips as you would a carrot. If the parsnip is large (more than 1-inch thick at its broad end), you must remove its woody core: Cut the thinner portion off and set it aside. Cut the thick portion in half and dig out the core with the end of a vegetable peeler, a paring knife, or a sharp spoon; the procedure is neither difficult nor time-consuming. *See page 100.*

Pasta Long pastas, like spaghetti and linguine, are best with sauces that don't have large chunks in them. Chunky sauces are best served with bigger, tube-shaped pasta, such as penne, rigatoni, or ziti, or with shells and elbows (all of which gather in the chunks). *See page 18.*

Don't change the type of sauce you're making because you don't have the "correct" pasta shape. If you make spaghetti with a chunky sauce, some of the sauce will stay at the bottom of the bowl. This is less than ideal, of course, but you can eat that sauce with a spoon, or some bread, and next time you shop you might remember to stock up on penne. *See page 18.*

The best quality pasta is made from 100% durum wheat. It is easier to keep from overcooking, has a deeper, more appealing color, and a texture that "grabs" the sauce better. It's made from 100% durum wheat. It may come from the United States, or from Italy—the difference in price can determine your preference, although Italian pasta is not expensive. Most experienced cooks choose Italian pasta, which is widely available. *See page 19.*

Peanut oil Peanut oil is not an all-purpose oil, but it's great for frying, and it's also wonderful when you want to give a distinctively Asian twist to almost anything. *See page 4.*

Peas To buy peas to shell, open a pod or two in the store; they should be full of medium-sized peas. Big peas can be tough, so taste a couple; if you want to keep eating, buy them. If the peas are large and tough, they will need to be cooked before eating. *See page 101.*

Store all peas, loosely wrapped in plastic, in the vegetable bin. But use them quickly; their sweetness is fleeting. *See page 101.*

To shell peas: With the flat end of the pea down, grasp the tip of the flower end and pull down, removing the string along the bottom of the pea. *See page 101.*

Pork Pork has become so lean that certain cuts—the tenderloin for example—have become practically tasteless. These days, the best cut for stir-fries and many other uses is the shoulder, which still contains enough fat to be flavorful. *See page 74.*

Pork chop A good pork chop contains some fat, and if you cannot find *center cut pork chops* that show some marbling, look for *shoulder* (also called *blade*) chops; *loin-end chops* are almost always too lean. Try to find chops that are at least an inch thick—you'll be much happier with one thick chop than two thin ones, which invariably overcook. *See page 72.*

Port You need not cook with vintage port, but you need a sweet wine of some body and integrity. A decent tawny port will do the trick, and will keep for as long as it takes you to use (or drink) the rest of the bottle. Oloroso sherry would also be good. *See page 60.*

Rice	The best rice for pilaf—and, generally speaking, the *ne plus ultra* of long-grain rice—is the wonderful Indian basmati, whose grains are even longer than that of other varieties, and whose nutty, beguiling aroma adds another dimension to cooking. *See page 84.*
Salmon	Farm-raised salmon ("Norwegian salmon," a widely used misnomer) is available year-round and is fairly flavorful and usually inexpensive. Wild salmon, from the Pacific Northwest, is only available fresh from spring to fall, but it's preferable, especially if you can find king (chinook), sockeye (red), or coho (silver). Chum and pink salmon are less valued but still good wild varieties. *See page 42.*
	The cooking time for salmon varies according to your taste. I prefer my salmon cooked to what might be called medium-rare to medium, with a well-cooked exterior and a fairly red center. So, I always look at the center of a piece of salmon to judge its doneness. Remember that fish retains enough heat to continue cooking after it has been removed from the heat source, so stop cooking just before the salmon reaches the point you'd consider it done. *See page 42.*
Sausage	Italian sausage is preferable freshly made in patties (most Italian markets have this, as do some supermarkets). If that's unavailable, use links of Italian sausage—hot or sweet—but remove the meat from its casing. Some of the new varieties of sausage, including those made from chicken or turkey, can be quite good, but those labeled "low-fat" are often "low-flavor," too. *See page 26.*
Scallops	The best scallops are either bay scallops (when available) or sea scallops. The least desirable (and of course the least expensive) are the tiny calicos, not much bigger than pencil erasers and just as rubbery when overcooked. *See page 27.*
	Many scallops are soaked in phosphates, which cause them to absorb water and lose flavor. Always buy scallops from someone you trust, and let him or her know that you want unsoaked (sometimes called "dry") scallops. *See page 27.*
Sesame oil	Dark sesame oil, sold in almost every Asian market and many supermarkets, is roasted, and completely different from ordinary "light" sesame oil, which is a simple, almost tasteless, cooking oil. Store dark sesame oil in the refrigerator, and use it for dressings, or at the end of stir-fries. *See page 40.*
	To add variety and flavor to stir-fries, try (alone or in combination): a teaspoon of dark sesame oil, ½ to 1 cup raw or roasted cashews or peanuts, or 1 cup chopped shallots. *See page 58.*
Soy sauce	When shopping for soy sauce, look for ingredients in this order: soy, wheat (wheat followed by soy is also acceptable), and salt. If the first ingredient is salt, and a chemical is listed in the ingredient list, it isn't real soy sauce. *See page 4.*
Spinach	Spinach leaves must be plump; any wilting or yellowing is a bad sign. Store it, loosely wrapped in plastic, in the vegetable bin, but use it as fast as you can. It will keep for a few days. Sold year-round, it's in season locally in cool but not cold or hot weather. *See page 22.*
	Wash spinach well, in several changes of water; it's sandy. Remove very thick stems, but leave thinner ones on; they'll be fine. Don't chop too finely before cooking, or you'll lose too many little pieces to the cooking liquid. *See page 22.*

Spinach	For a dish like pasta with cream and spinach, frozen spinach is almost as good as fresh. Thaw it first, squeeze out excess liquid, and proceed (it's likely to have been chopped already). *See page 22.*
Steak	*Strip steaks* are usually sold boneless and make the ideal individual steaks. *Rib-eyes*, the boneless center of the rib, are also very tender and very flavorful, and make good individual steaks. *Skirt steaks*, if you can find them (actually the steer's diaphragm), are great steaks, though they become extremely tough if cooked beyond medium-rare. *See page 64.*
	Use a skillet that will fit the steaks comfortably, without either crowding them (which will cause them to steam rather than brown) or leaving too much room, which will allow the butter to burn. *See page 66.*
Wine	Any wine you use in cooking should be good enough to drink. It need not be expensive or esoteric, but neither should it be the so-called "cooking wine" sold in supermarkets. Decent red wine makes a difference here; zinfandel, for example, has a spicy fruitiness that complements tarragon and shallots nicely. *See page 66.*
	Lamb sautéed with wine is a dish in which good red wine will stand out. As always, cook with something you would like to drink, but in the case of lamb—especially if the amount is small—try to use something with real character—a good Bordeaux or other Cabernet will make a huge difference in the sauce. *See page 78.*

Index

A

Almonds
  buttered, salmon roasted with, 42
  in Curried Chicken Salad, 61
Anchovies
  in Braised Broccoli with Garlic and Wine, 95
  shopping tip, 95
Apples
  in Curried Chicken Salad, 61
  pork chops with, 73
  sautéed, 106
Arugula and Blue Cheese Salad, 2
Asian menus, 112
Asparagus
  crisp-cooked, 94
  illustrations on preparing, *94*

B

Bacon
  greens with, 5
  pasta with onion and, 24
  shopping tip, 5
Balsamic vinegar
  preparation tip, 108
  shopping tip, 108
  strawberries with, 108
Bananas, sautéed, 106
Basil
  corn, tomato, and zucchini soup with, 12
  stir-fried spicy beef with, 68
Bean(s)
  black, sauce, chicken wings with, 59
  black, soup, 13
  black, and rice, Spanish-style, 91
  black, stir-fried beef with tomatoes and, 67
  black, with crisp pork and orange, 90

burritos with meat, 81
red, twice-cooked ("refried"), with cumin, 88
refried, traditional, 88
soup, additions to, 13
and tomato casserole, 89
Beef
  cooking tip, 69
  ground, in Bean Burritos with Meat, 81
  salad with mint, 69
  shopping tip, 64
  steak, broiled, 65
  steak, grilled, 64
  steak, pan-grilled, 65
  steak, pan-seared, with red wine sauce, 66
  steak, Tuscan, 65
  stir-fried spicy, with basil, 68
  stir-fried, with onions, 67
  stir-fried, with tomatoes and black beans, 67
Black bean(s)
  with crisp pork and orange, 90
  and rice, Spanish-style, 91
  sauce, chicken wings with, 59
  soup, 13
  stir-fried beef with tomatoes and, 67
Blue cheese, arugula and, salad, 2
Braised Broccoli with Garlic and Wine, 95
Bread crumbs
  in Roast Rack of Lamb with Persillade, 79
  in Roast Shrimp with Tomatoes, 45
Broccoli
  braised, with garlic and wine, 95
  pasta with, 20
  stir-fried chicken with, 58
Broiled Chicken with Lemon and Herbs, 52

Broiled Chicken with Pesto, 52
Broiled Chicken Cutlets, 53
  with herb marinade, 53
  in sweet soy marinade, 53
Broiled Flatfish or Other Thin White Fillets, 34
  with garlic-parsley sauce, 35
  with mustard and herbs, 35
Broiled Lamb Chops, 77
  Italian-Style, 77
Broiled Shrimp, My Way, 43
Broiled Steak, 65
Broth, shopping tip, 14
Brunch menus, 113
Burgers, lamb, with smoked mozzarella, 80
Burritos, bean, with meat, 81
Butter
  fettuccine with spinach, cream, and, 22
  garlic, 51
  quick-braised carrots with, 96
  salmon roasted in, 42
Buttered Peas, 101
Buttery Scallops, 46

C

Cabbage
  and carrot salad with soy-lime dressing, 4
  illustrations on coring and shredding, *4*
Cake, noodle, crisp pan-fried, 31
Carrot(s)
  cabbage and, salad, with soy-lime dressing, 4
  quick-braised, with butter, 96
  quick-braised, with orange and ginger, 96
Casserole, bean and tomato, 89
Casual dinner party menus, 113
Cauliflower, stir-fried chicken with, 58

Chard
    shopping tip, 97
    with Pine Nuts and Currants, 97
Cheese. *See also* Parmesan cheese
    blue, arugula and, salad, 2
    dressing, quick, 3
    feta, shrimp with, 44
    Gorgonzola sauce, creamy, ziti with, 21
    quesadillas, 9
    shopping tips, 21, 23
Chicken
    breast, cooking tips, 53, 54
    breasts, crunchy curried, 55
    broiled or grilled, with pesto, 52
    cutlets, grilled or broiled, 53
    cutlets, herb-roasted, 54
    cutlets, sautéed, 52
    cutlets, sesame-coated, 52
    cutlets, spice-coated, 52
    ground, in Bean Burritos with Meat, 81
    in lemon sauce, 56
    preparation tip, 50
    salad, curried, 61
    salad with walnuts, 60
    satay, 57
    shopping tips, 50, 60
    soup, quick, with rice or noodles, 14
    stir-fried, with broccoli or cauliflower, 58
    wings, preparation tip, 59
    wings with black bean sauce, 59
Chickpeas with Lemon, 87
Chile Oil, 51
Chocolate Mousse, 111
Clams
    linguine with, 28
    preparation tips, 29
    shopping tips, 29

Cod, sautéed, 38
    extra-crisp, 38
Cold Noodles with Sesame or Peanut
    Sauce, 30
Collards
    illustrations on preparing, *11*
    shopping tip, 11
Cookies, oatmeal, 110
    lacy, 110
Cooking basics, viii–xi
    equipment, x–xi
    food safety, ix–x
    techniques, x
    time, viii–ix
Corn
    garlicky or spicy grilled or roasted, 98
    grilled or roasted, 98
    illustrations on preparing, *98*
    tomato, and zucchini soup with basil, 12
Cornmeal, in Sautéed Chicken Cutlets, 52
Cream, fettucine with spinach, butter,
    and, 22
Cream of Mushroom Soup, 10
Crisp-Cooked Asparagus, 94
Crisp Pan-Fried Noodle Cake, 31
Crunchy Curried Chicken Breasts, 55
Crust, sesame, sautéed flatfish with, 36
Cumin, twice-cooked ("refried") beans
    with, 88
Currants, chard with pine nuts and, 97
Curry(ied)
    chicken breasts, crunchy, 55
    chicken salad, 61
    powder, shopping tips, 55, 61
    sautéed flatfish or other thin white with
        lime and, 37

D
Desserts, 104–11
Dressing
    blue cheese, quick, 3
    soy-lime, cabbage and carrot salad with, 4
Duck salad with walnuts, 60

E
Easy Waffles with Ice Cream, 109
Eggs
    frittata, 8
    omelets, 6–7
Egg noodle cake, crisp pan-fried, 31
Elegant lunch and dinner menus, 113
Entertaining, quick dishes great for, 65
Extra-Crisp Sautéed Cod or Other Thick
    White Fillets, 38

F
Fall menus, 113
Fermented black beans, shopping tip, 59
Feta cheese, shrimp with, 44
Fettucine with Spinach, Butter, and Cream, 22
Fish. *See also specific types*
    shopping tip, 14
    soup, lightning-quick, 15
Fish fillets
    broiled, four quick ideas for, 35
    cooking tips, 34, 36
    in packages with spinach, 39
    preparation tip, 36
    removing pin bones, *42*
    thick white, sautéed, 38
    thick white, sautéed, extra-crisp, 38
    thick white, shopping tip, 38
    thick white, variety of, 38
    thin white, broiled, 34
    thin white, sautéed, 36

thin white, sautéed, curry and lime, 36

thin white, sautéed, with sesame crust 36

thin white, sautéed, with soy sauce, 36

thin white, variety of, 37

steaks, poached, with vegetables and mustard sauce, 41

steaks, poached, with vegetables, 41

Flatfish

broiled, 34

sautéed, 36

sautéed, with curry and lime, 37

sautéed, with sesame crust, 36

sautéed, with soy sauce 36

Fried Rice with Greens, 86

Frittata, 8

herb, 8

vegetable, 8

Fudge, hot, 109

G

Garlic

butter, 51

braised broccoli with wine and, 95

Garlicky or Spicy Grilled or Roasted Corn, 98

parsley sauce, broiled flatfish or other thin white fillets with, 35

sautéed mushrooms with, 99

sherry-, sauce, pork chops with, 73

Ginger

quick-braised carrots with orange and, 96

scallops, 46

stir-fried pork with snow peas and, 75

Gorgonzola sauce, creamy, ziti with, 21

Great Green Salad, 2

Greens. See also Salad(s)

with bacon, 5

in Bean Burritos with Meat, 81

fried rice with, 86

in Grilled Mesclun-Stuffed Tuna or Swordfish Steaks, 40

shopping tip, 2

tender, warm salad of scallops and, 47

Grilled chicken with pesto, 52

Grilled corn, spicy, 98

Grilled Lamb Chops, Italian-Style, 77

Grilled Mesclun-Stuffed Tuna or Swordfish Steaks, 40

Grilled or Broiled Chicken Cutlets, 53

in sweet soy marinade, 53

with herb marinade, 53

Grilled or Broiled Lamb Chops, 77

Grilled or Roasted Corn, 98

Grilled Steak, 64

H

Halibut

poached, with vegetables, 41

poached, with vegetables and mustard sauce, 41

Herb(s)

broiled flatfish or other thin white fillets with mustard and, 35

broiled or grilled chicken with lemon and, 52

fresh, rice with, 85

frittata, 8

marinade, grilled or broiled chicken cutlets with, 53

-roasted chicken cutlets, 54

salmon roasted with, 42

shopping tip, 85

Hot Fudge, 109

I

Ice cream, easy waffles with, 109

Illustrations

asparagus, preparing, 94

cabbage, coring and shredding, 4

corn, preparing, 98

kale and collards, preparing, 11

onions, preparing, 25

pin bones, removing, 42

shrimp, preparing, 43

tomatoes, preparing, 12

Italian menus, 112

Italian sausage

sautéed, with peppers and, 71

shopping tip, 26

Italian-style, broiled or grilled lamb chops, 77

K

Kale

and potato soup, 11

and potato soup with linguica, 11

illustrations on preparing, 11

shopping tip, 11

L

Lacy Oatmeal Cookies, 110

Lamb

burgers, with smoked mozzarella, 80

chops, grilled or broiled, 77

ground, cooking tip, 80

medallions with shallots, tarragon, and red wine, 78

rack of, roast, with persillade, 79

shopping tip, 79

Lemon

broiled or grilled chicken with herbs and, 52

chickpeas with, 87

sauce, chicken in, 56

sautéed medallions of pork with parsley and, 76

Lightning-Quick Fish Soup, 15
Lime
  sautéed flatfish or other thin white fillets
    with curry and, 37
  soy-, dressing, cabbage and carrot salad
    with, 4
Linguica, kale and potato soup with, 11
Linguine with Clams, 28
Linguine with Scallops, 27
Low-carbohydrate menus, 112

M
"Marinara", shrimp, 44
Marinade
  herb, grilled or broiled chicken cutlets
    with, 53
  soy, sweet, grilled or broiled chicken
    cutlets in, 53
Meat. *See also specific types*
  bean burritos with, 81
Medallions of pork, sautéed, with lemon and
    parsley, 76
Medallions, lamb, with shallots, tarragon,
    and red wine, 78
Mediterranean menus, 112
Menus
  quick, 112–13
  20 minutes or less recipes, 114–15
Mesclun-stuffed tuna, grilled, or swordfish
    steaks, 40
Mexican menus, 112
Microwaved or Simmered Sweet Potatoes, 103
Mint, beef salad with, 69
Moors and Christians, 91
Mousse, chocolate, 111
Mozzarella, lamburgers with smoked, 80
Mushroom(s)
  omelet, 7
  soup, 10

  soup, cream of, 10
  preparation tips, 10
  sautéed, with garlic, 99
  varieties, 99
Mustard, Dijon
  broiled flatfish or other thin white fillets
    with herbs and, 35
  poached halibut or other fish steaks with
    vegetables and, 41
  pork chops with, 73

N
Nam pla
  in Beef Salad with Mint, 69
  in Chicken Satay, 57
  shopping tip, 68
  in Stir-Fried Spicy Beef with Basil, 68
Noodles
  cold, with sesame or peanut sauce, 30
  egg, cake, crisp pan-fried, 31
  quick chicken soup with, 14
  thick chicken soup with, 14
Nuts
  pine, chard with, and currants, 97
  pine, pilaf with raisins and, 84
  walnuts, chicken or duck salad with, 60

O
Oatmeal Cookies, 110
  lacy, 110
Oil, chile, 51
Omelet, 6
  cooking tip, 6
  five quick fillings for, 7
  mushroom, 7
  Spanish, 7
Onion(s)
  illustrations on preparing, 25
  pasta with bacon and, 24

  pork chops with peppers and, 73
  sautéed Italian sausage with peppers
    and, 71
  stir-fried beef with, 67
  sweet, stir-fried pork with, 75
  tomato-, salsa, 81
Orange
  black beans with crisp pork and, 90
  flavor, spicy, shrimp with, 43
  quick-braised carrots with ginger and, 96

P
Packages, red snapper or other fillets in,
    with spinach, 39
Pancetta, in Pasta with Onion and
    Bacon, 24
Pan-fried noodle cake, crisp, 31
Pan-Grilled Steak, 65
Pan-Seared Steak with Red Wine Sauce, 66
Parmesan cheese
  in Fettucine with Spinach, Butter, and
    Cream, 22
  in Frittata, 8
  in Pasta with Sausage, 26
  penne with ricotta, peas, and, 23
  shopping tips, 23
  veal cutlets with rosemary and, 70
  in Ziti with Creamy Gorgonzola
    Sauce, 21
Parsley
  garlic-, sauce, broiled flatfish or other thin
    white fillets with, 35
  sautéed medallions of pork with
    lemon, 76
Parsnips
  preparation tip, 100
  pureed, 100
  shopping tip, 100

Pasta. *See also specific types*
   with Broccoli, 20
   cooking tip, 18
   noodles, cold, with sesame or peanut sauce, 30
   noodles, egg, cake, crisp pan-fried, 31
   noodles, quick chicken soup with, 14
   noodles, thick chicken soup with, 14
   with Onion and Bacon, 24
   with Raw Tomato Sauce, 19
   with Sausage, 26
   shopping tip, 19
   with tomato sauce, 18
Peanut oil, shopping tip, 4
Peanut sauce, cold noodles with, 30
Peas
   buttered, 101
   chickpeas with lemon, 87
   penne with ricotta, Parmesan, and, 23
   preparation tip, 101
   shopping tip, 101
   snow, stir-fried pork with ginger and, 75
Penne with Ricotta, Parmesan, and Peas, 23
Peppers
   in Black Beans and Rice, Spanish Style, 91
   in Western Omelet, 7
   pork chops with onions and, 73
   sautéed Italian sausage with onions and, 71
Persillade, roast rack of lamb with, 79
Pesto, 51
   broiled or grilled chicken with, 52
Pilaf
   with Raisins and Pine Nuts, 84
   rice, 84
Pin bones, removing, *42*

Pine nuts
   chard with, and currants, 97
   pilaf with raisins and, 84
Poached Halibut or Other Fish Steaks with Vegetables, 41
Poached Halibut or Other Steaks with Vegetables and Mustard Sauce, 41
Pork. *See also* Linguica; Sausage
   chops, sautéed, 72
   chops, shopping tip, 72
   chops with apples, 73
   chops with mustard, 73
   chops with onions and peppers, 73
   chops with sherry-garlic sauce, 73
   crisp, black beans with orange and, 90
   medallions of, sautéed, with lemon and parsley, 76
   shopping tip, 74
   stir-fried, with spinach, 74
   stir-fries, quick additions to, 75
Port, shipping tip, 60
Potato(es)
   kale and, soup, 11
   kale and, soup, with linguica, 11
   sweet, microwaved or simmered, 103
Poultry, 48–61
Pureed Parsnips, 100

Q
Quesadillas, cheese, 9
Quick Blue Cheese Dressing, 3
Quick Chicken Soup with Rice or Noodles, 14
Quick menus, 112–13
Quick-Braised Carrots with Butter, 96
Quick-Braised Carrots with Orange and Ginger, 96

R
Rack of lamb, roast, with persillade, 79
Raspberry Fool, 107
Red Snapper or Other Fillets in Packages with Spinach, 39
Red wine. *See also* Wine
   shopping tip, 78
Refried beans, traditional, 88
"Refried" beans with cumin, 88
Rice
   black beans and, Spanish-style, 91
   with Fresh Herbs, 85
   fried, with greens, 86
   pilaf, 84
   quick chicken soup with, 14
   shopping tip, 84
   thick chicken soup with, 14
Ricotta, penne with Parmesan, peas, and, 23
Roast Rack of Lamb with Persillade, 79
Roast Shrimp with Tomatoes, 45
Roasted corn, 98
Rosemary, veal cutlets with Parmesan and, 70

S
Salad(s)
   arugula and blue cheese, 2
   beef, with mint, 69
   cabbage and carrot, with soy-lime dressing, 4
   chicken or duck, with walnuts, 60
   chicken, curried, 61
   five quick additions to, 2
   great green, 2
   Greek, simple, 2
   Greens with Bacon, 5
   warm, of scallops and tender greens, 47

Salmon Roasted in Butter, 42

Salmon Roasted with Buttered Almonds, 42

Salmon Roasted with Herbs, 42

Salsa, tomato-onion, 81

Satay, chicken, 57

Sauce

    black bean, chicken wings with, 59

    Gorgonzola, creamy, ziti with, 21

    lemon, chicken in, 56

    mustard, poached halibut or other fish
        steaks with vegetables and, 41

    pasta, cooking tip, 18

    red wine, pan-seared steak with, 66

    sherry-garlic, pork chops with, 73

    soy, sautéed flatfish or other thin white
        fillets with 36

    tomato, pasta with, 18

    tomato, raw, pasta with, 19

Sausage

    in Black Beans with Crisp Pork and
        Orange, 90

    Italian, sautéed, with peppers and
        onions, 71

    linguica, kale and potato soup with, 11

    pasta with, 26

    shopping, tip, 26

Sautéed Apples, 106

Sautéed Bananas, 106

Sautéed Chicken Cutlets, 52

Sautéed Cod or Other Thick White Fillets, 38

    extra-crisp, 38

Sautéed Flatfish or Other Thin White
    Fillets, 36

    with curry and lime, 37

    with sesame crust, 37

    with soy sauce, 37

Sautéed Italian Sausage with Peppers and
    Onions, 71

Sautéed Medallions of Pork with Lemon
    and Parsley, 76

Sautéed Mushrooms with Garlic, 99

Sautéed Pork Chops, 72

Sautéed Scallops, 46

Sautéed Summer Squash or Zucchini, 102

Scallops

    buttery, 46

    ginger, 46

    linguine with, 27

    sautéed, 46

    shopping tips, 27

    warm salad of, and tender greens, 47

"Scampi", shrimp, 43

Sesame-Coated Chicken Cutlets, 52

Sesame crust, sautéed flatfish with, 36

Sesame oil, shopping tip, 40

Sesame sauce, cold noodles with, 30

Sesame seeds, toasted, 86

Shallots, lamb medallions with tarragon,
    red wine, and, 78

Sherry-garlic sauce, pork chops with, 73

Shrimp

    broiled, my way, 43

    with Feta Cheese, 44

    illustrations on preparing, *43*

    "Marinara", 44

    roast, with tomatoes, 45

    "Scampi", 43

    with Spicy Orange Flavor, 43

Simmered sweet potatoes, 103

Simple Greek Salad, 2

Slab bacon, shopping tip, 5

Snow peas, stir-fried pork with ginger and, 75

Soup

    black bean, 13

    chicken, quick, with rice or noodles, 14

chicken, thick, with rice or noodles, 14

corn, tomato, and zucchini, with basil, 12

cream of mushroom, 10

fish, lightning-quick, 15

kale and potato, 11

kale and potato, with linguica, 11

mushroom, 10

Soy sauce

    -lime dressing, cabbage and carrot salad
        with, 4

    marinade, sweet, grilled or broiled chicken
        cutlets in, 53

    sautéed flatfish or other thin white fillets
        with 36

    shopping tip, 4

Spanish Omelet, 7

Spanish-style, black beans and rice, 91

Spice-Coated Chicken Cutlets, 52

Spicy Grilled Corn, 98

Spinach

    fettucine with butter, cream, and, 22

    preparation tips, 22

    red snapper or other fillets in packages
        with, 39

    shopping tip

    stir-fried pork with, 74

Squash, summer, sautéed, 102

Steak, beef

    broiled, 65

    cooking tip, 66

    pan-grilled, 65

    pan-seared, with red wine sauce, 66

    shopping tip, 64

    Tuscan, 65

Steaks, swordfish, grilled mesclun-stuffed, 40

Stir-fries

    pork, quick additions to, 75

    preparation tip, 59

Stir-Fried Beef with Onions, 67

Stir-Fried Beef with Tomatoes and Black Beans, 67

Stir-Fried Chicken with Broccoli or Cauliflower, 58

Stir-Fried Pork with Snow Peas and Ginger, 75

Stir-Fried Pork with Spinach, 74

Stir-Fried Pork with Sweet Onions, 75

Stir-Fried Spicy Beef with Basil, 68

Strawberries with Balsamic Vinegar, 108

Summer menus, 113

Sweet potatoes, microwaved or simmered, 103

Swordfish steaks, grilled mesclun-stuffed, 40

T

Tarragon
   cooking tip, 39
   lamb medallions with shallots, tarragon, and, 78

Thick Chicken Soup with Rice or Noodles, 14

Tips reference, 116–22

Toasted Sesame Seeds, 86

Tomato(es)
   in Black Beans and Rice, Spanish Style, 91
   casserole, bean and, 89
   corn, and zucchini soup with basil, 12
   illustrations on preparing, *12*
   -Onion Salsa, 81
   in Pasta with Onion and Bacon, 24
   roast shrimp with, 45
   sauce, pasta with, 18
   sauce, raw, pasta with, 19
   sauce, three ways to vary, 18
   stir-fried beef with black beans and, 67

Tortillas, in Bean Burritos with Meat, 81

Traditional Refried Beans, 88

Tuna, grilled mesclun-stuffed, 40

Turkey, ground, in Bean Burritos with Meat, 81

Tuscan Steak, 65

20 minute recipes
   Arugula and Blue Cheese Salad, 2
   Braised Broccoli with Garlic and Wine, 95
   Broiled Flatfish or Other Thin White Fillets, 34
   Broiled Flatfish or Other Thin White Fillets with Garlic-Parsley Sauce, 35
   Broiled Flatfish or Other Thin White Fillets with Mustard and Herbs, 35
   Broiled Steak, 65
   Buttered Peas, 101
   Buttery Scallops, 46
   Cabbage and Carrot Salad with Soy-Lime Dressing, 4
   Cheese Quesadillas, 9
   Chile Oil, 51
   Crunchy Curried Chicken Breasts, 55
   Extra-Crisp Sautéed Cod or Other Thick White Fillets, 38
   Fried Rice with Greens, 86
   Garlic Butter, 51
   Ginger Scallops, 46
   Great Green Salad, 2
   Hot Fudge, 109
   Lamb Medallions with Shallots, Tarragon, and Red Wine, 78
   Lightning-Quick Fish Soup, 15
   Mushroom Omelet, 7
   Omelet, 6
   Pan-Grilled Steak, 65
   Pan-Seared Steak with Red Wine Sauce, 66
   Pasta with Tomato Sauce, 18

Pesto, 51

Quick Blue Cheese Dressing, 3

Quick-Braised Carrots with Butter, 96

Quick-Braised Carrots with Orange and Ginger, 96

Raspberry Fool, 107

Salmon Roasted in Butter, 42

Salmon Roasted with Buttered Almonds, 42

Salmon Roasted with Herbs, 42

Sautéed Chicken Cutlets, 52

Sautéed Cod or Other Thick White Fillets, 38

Sautéed Flatfish or Other Thin White Fillets, 36

Sautéed Flatfish or Other Thin White Fillets with Curry and Lime, 37

Sautéed Flatfish or Other Thin White Fillets with Sesame Crust, 37

Sautéed Flatfish or Other Thin White Fillets with Soy Sauce, 37

Sautéed Medallions of Pork with Lemon and Parsley, 76

Sautéed Mushrooms with Garlic, 99

Sautéed Scallops, 46

Sesame-Coated Chicken Cutlets, 52

Shrimp "Marinara", 44

Shrimp with Feta Cheese, 44

Simple Greek Salad, 2

Spanish Omelet, 7

Spice-Coated Chicken Cutlets, 52

Stir-Fried Pork with Snow Peas and Ginger, 75

Stir-Fried Pork with Spinach, 74

Stir-Fried Pork with Sweet Onions, 75

Strawberries with Balsamic Vinegar, 108

Tomato-Onion Salsa, 81

Toasted Sesame Seeds, 86

Traditional Refried Beans, 88

20 minute recipes *(cont.)*
    Tuscan Steak, 65
    Twice-Cooked ("Refried") Beans with
        Cumin, 88
    Vinaigrette, 3
    Warm Salad of Scallops and Tender
        Greens, 47
    Western Omelet, 7
Twice-Cooked ("Refried") Beans with
    Cumin, 88

V
Veal cutlets
    1950s-Style, 70
    with rosemary and Parmesan, 70
Vegetable(s). *See also specific types*
    frittata, 8
    poached halibut or other fish steaks with
        mustard sauce and, 41

Vegetarian menus, 112
Vinaigrette, 3
Vinegar, balsamic, strawberries with, 108

W
Waffles, easy, with ice cream, 109
Walnuts, chicken or duck salad with, 60
Warm Salad of Scallops and Tender
    Greens, 47
Weekend family menus, 112
Weeknight family menus, 112
Western Omelet, 7
Wine
    red, in Black Beans with Crisp Pork
        and Orange, 90
    red, sauce, pan-seared steak with, 66
    red, shallots, tarragon, and, lamb
        medallions with, 78
    shopping tip, 66

sweet, in Chicken or Duck Salad with
    Walnuts, 60
white, in Braised Broccoli with Garlic
    and Wine, 95
white, in Chicken in Lemon Sauce, 56
white, in Grilled Mesclun-Stuffed Tuna
    or Swordfish Steaks, 40
white, in Linguine with Clams, 28
white, in Sautéed Medallions of Pork
    with Lemon and Parsley, 76
white, in Sautéed Pork Chops, 72

Z
Ziti with Creamy Gorgonzola Sauce, 21
Zucchini
    corn, and tomato soup, with basil, 12
    sautéed, 102

Conversions, Substitutions, and Helpful Hints

Cooking at High Altitudes

Every increase in elevation brings a decrease in air pressure, which results in a lower boiling point. At 7,000 feet, for example—the altitude of many towns in the Southwest—water boils at 199°F. This means slower cooking times (and makes a pressure cooker a more desirable appliance). Families who have been living in the mountains for years have already discovered, through trial and error, the best ways to adjust.

Newcomers to high altitudes must be patient and experiment to discover what works best. But here are some general rules for high-altitude cooking:

1. For stove-top cooking, use higher heat when practical; extend cooking times as necessary. Beans and grains will require significantly more time than at sea level.

2. Assume that batters and doughs will rise faster than at sea level.

3. Over 3,000 feet, increase baking temperatures by 25 degrees.

4. Over 3,000 feet, reduce baking powder (or other leavening) measurements by about 10 percent; increase liquid in baked goods by the same percentage. You may want to reduce the amount of sugar slightly as well.

5. For every 2,000-foot increase in altitude above 3,000 feet, reduce leavening even further.

Imperial Measurements

Theoretically, both the United Kingdom and Canada use the metric system, but older recipes rely on the "imperial" measurement system, which differs from standard U.S. measurements in its liquid ("fluid") measurements:

> $\frac{1}{4}$ cup = 2.5 ounces
>
> $\frac{1}{2}$ cup ("gill") = 5 ounces
>
> 1 cup = 10 ounces
>
> 1 pint = 20 ounces
>
> 1 quart = 40 ounces

Some Useful Substitutions

> 1 cup cake flour = $\frac{7}{8}$ cup all-purpose flour + $\frac{1}{8}$ cup cornstarch
>
> 1 tablespoon baking powder = 2 teaspoons baking soda + 1 teaspoon cream of tartar
>
> 1 cup buttermilk = 1 scant cup milk at room temperature + 1 tablespoon white vinegar
>
> 1 cup brown sugar = 1 cup white sugar + 2 tablespoons molasses
>
> 1 cup sour cream = 1 cup yogurt (preferably full fat)

Measurement Conversions

Note that volume (i.e., cup) measures and weight (i.e., ounce) measures convert perfectly for liquids only. Solids are a different story; 1 cup of flour weighs only 4 or 5 ounces.

> Dash or pinch = less than $\frac{1}{4}$ teaspoon
>
> 3 teaspoons = 1 tablespoon
>
> 2 tablespoons = 1 fluid ounce
>
> 4 tablespoons = $\frac{1}{4}$ cup = 2 fluid ounces
>
> 16 tablespoons = 1 cup = 8 fluid ounces
>
> 2 cups = 1 pint
>
> 2 pints = 1 quart
>
> 4 quarts = 1 gallon

Imperial vs. Metric

These are approximate, but are fine for all uses.

> 1 ounce = 28 grams
>
> 1 pound = 500 grams or $\frac{1}{2}$ kilo
>
> 2.2 pounds = 1 kilo
>
> 1 teaspoon = 5 milliliters (ml)
>
> 1 tablespoon = 15 milliliters
>
> 1 cup = $\frac{1}{4}$ liter
>
> 1 quart = 1 liter

Doneness Temperatures

Use an instant-read thermometer for the best possible accuracy; always measure with the probe in the thickest part of the meat, not touching any bone (ideally, measure in more than one place). When you gain experience in cooking, you'll be able to judge doneness by look and feel.

Beef

125°F = Rare

130–135°F = Medium-rare

135–140°F = Medium

140–150°F = Medium-well

155°F + = Well-done

Pork

137°F = Temperature at which trichinosis is killed

150°F = slightly pink but moist

160°F = Well-done (and probably dry)

Chicken

160°F = Breast is done

165°F = Thigh is done

Lamb

125°F = Very rare

130°F = Rare

135°F = Medium-rare

140°F = Medium

150°F = Medium-well

160°F + = Well-done

USDA—Recommended Internal Temperatures

The recommended internal temperatures given in this book for meats and poultry are based on producing the best-tasting food, and are in line with traditional levels of doneness. The United States Department of Agriculture (USDA), however, generally recommends higher temperatures, which reduces the potential danger of contracting illness caused by bacteria.

Beef, Veal, and Lamb

Ground meat (hamburger, etc.) 160°F

Roasts, Steaks, and Chops

145°F = Medium-rare

160°F = Medium

170°F = Well-done

Pork (all cuts including ground)

160°F = Medium

170°F = Well-done

Poultry

Ground chicken and turkey: 165°F

Whole chicken and turkey: 180°F

Stuffing: 165°F

Poultry Breasts: 170°F

Poultry Thighs: Cook until juices run clear

Egg Dishes: 160°F